AF251163

Breakthrough WORSHIP

"Cynthia, you have done a super job with this book! And it all comes out of your seeking Him, His presence, and seeking to please Him. You have had quite a journey…Thank you, thank you, thank you! I started reading your manuscript this morning…It is truly amazing! I could feel the excitement of the Holy Spirit within as I read the pages. You have truly captured the essence of worship…Amen, Amen, and Amen!…Not surprising that the Lord told you to write this book!…it is apparent that God has prepared you to write such a book…It is wonderful!"

—CAROL GRIFFITH
PRISON MINISTRY, BUDAPEST, HUNGARY

"Wow this is awesome…you are simply a wonderful writer and such love for the Lord pours through what you have written…I thought it was very well done and you have set out how to worship in a corporate setting and brought the reader into the fullness of that experience. It is an easy read and something that will be useful to the Bride. Well done my sister! You can see your heart for God and worship; it is beautiful!…I can't wait to see this in print!"

—SUSAN CARROLL
ATTORNEY, PANAMA CITY, FLORIDA

"[T]he book is excellent…[a] masterpiece…[It] is well written and the content explains beautifully the ministry of prophetic worship which I can see you have learned over many years of personal experience. You are not dogmatic in your opinions, leaving room for others to have their own angle on things, and you have introduced many personal examples which is rather like punctuating your text with pictures. Well done!…I believe the book is really instructive, edifying, upbuilding, and even corrective in nature. Ten out of ten, Cynthia…You really have done an excellent job…May this book be used to bless people all around the globe."

—ANDREW BAKER
FOUNDER, PRESIDENT, ARK RESOURCES
SWITZERLAND AND UK

"...I am up in the wee hours of the morning! I couldn't stop reading your manuscript once I really had undivided time...As usual, I found it very informative and insightful. Your format is cohesive and easily followed. It follows a logical progression which makes the book an easier read. If a question popped into my head it was almost immediately addressed and I am a big proponent of that kind of writing...That is one of the things that I like about how you write: you don't leave me with questions hanging or loose ends. I found that the book was also challenging to me personally. It made me painfully and keenly aware of my shortcomings in the area of intercessory prayer and the need for more worship during my personal devotions...Your book has made me take a look at worship in a different light...[M]y preliminary assessment of your book is that it is spot on. I sense a great sincerity and desire to direct people to our Father through worship that ushers us into the glory realm...[T]he book has a powerful message for today's believers about worship and intercession. Your books are always meat and potatoes and not fluff sandwiches...I want something that will be helpful to me and change the way I think and act. Your books do that!...Please publish your book so that others can learn more about worship."

—Elizabeth Blaise
Prayer Ministry and Worship Teams
First Assembly of God, Plattsburgh, NY

Breakthrough WORSHIP

Piercing the Heavens to Impact the Earth

How to move together in
PROPHETIC INTERCESSION

DR. CYNTHIA D. WALLACE

CREATION
HOUSE

BREAKTHROUGH WORSHIP: PIERCING THE HEAVENS TO IMPACT THE EARTH — HOW TO MOVE TOGETHER IN PROPHETIC INTERCESSION by Dr. Cynthia D. Wallace
Published by Creation House
A Charisma Media Company
600 Rinehart Road
Lake Mary, Florida 32746
www.charismamedia.com

This book or parts thereof may not be reproduced in any form, stored in a retrieval system, or transmitted in any form by any means—electronic, mechanical, photocopy, recording, or otherwise—without prior written permission of the publisher, except as provided by United States of America copyright law.

Unless otherwise noted, all Scripture quotations are from the King James Version of the Bible.

Scripture quotations marked ESV are from the Holy Bible, English Standard Version. Copyright © 2001 by Crossway Bibles, a division of Good News Publishers. Used by permission.

Design Director: Justin Evans
Cover design by Karen Gonsalves

Copyright © 2015 by Dr. Cynthia D. Wallace
All rights reserved.

Visit the author's website: DrCDWallace.com.

Library of Congress Cataloging-in-Publication Data:
2014953366
International Standard Book Number: 978-1-62998-405-6
E-book International Standard Book Number:
978-1-62998-406-3

While the author has made every effort to provide accurate telephone numbers and Internet addresses at the time of publication, neither the publisher nor the author assumes any responsibility for errors or for changes that occur after publication.

First edition

15 16 17 18 19 — 987654321
Printed in the United States of America

DEDICATION

To my mother—in her hundredth year of life—who brought me up on the Bible and in the fear and admonition of the Lord. She imparted to me her wisdom, which has never departed from me.

> She openeth her mouth with wisdom; and in her tongue is the law of kindness. She looketh well to the ways of her household, and eateth not the bread of idleness. Her children arise up, and call her blessed; her husband also, and he praiseth her.
>
> —Proverbs 31:26–28

Her husband, my beloved father, has preceded her to glory, after seventy-eight years of devoted love and holy matrimony, and will surely be crowding the heavenly gates to be the first to welcome her home when the appointed time comes for their joyous reunion.

CONTENTS

ACKNOWLEDGMENTS

For DEVOTING VALUABLE time and insightful thought to reading and commenting on my manuscript, I am deeply indebted and most grateful to Andrew Baker, Susan Carroll, Carol Griffith, and Elizabeth Blaise—all of whose depth and purity of spirit I know and trust unreservedly

For his added objective and professional touch toward the fine tuning of my manuscript, I am beholden to my long-time friend Tom Cameron, who also asked the right questions for the clarification of any lingering ambiguities.

THE CALL TO WORSHIP

*...put off thy shoes from off thy feet, for the
place whereon thou standest is holy ground*

—Exodus 3:5 (see also Joshua 5:15)

Worship is sweeping the earth! Do you hear it?
The Holy Spirit is awakening an orchestra—
a global orchestra of worship. New waves of worship are
flowing out from the throne of heaven and being released
into the atmosphere. Listen! It's the call to true worshippers—the call to the bride—to come closer, to go deeper,
to rise higher. It is resounding all over the earth. Jesus is
calling His bride to come into the holy place—to become
one with Him.

This rising crescendo in preparation and anticipation
of Jesus's soon return is ushering in an atmosphere of
heaven to ease the transition from the earthly to the heavenly when He comes in the air to receive His bride unto
Himself. We might otherwise be shattered by our sudden
encounter with the brightness and purity of His Person.

God the Holy Spirit is acting in response to God the
Father and God the Son who seeks passionately to awaken

worship in the hearts of His people. Our God is searching throughout the whole earth for hearts of worship.

Wherever God has placed you, you are strategic. He has chosen you to break open a well of worship in that place—your city, your region, your country, and beyond, on out to the nations of the earth. He has exhorted us to bless and pray for the city to which we have been sent (see Jeremiah 29:7). You may be the one chosen by God to establish a powerful place of intercessory worship for spiritual breakthrough in your city.

The first time I received a prophetic word that I was going to write a book on worship, I rejected it out of hand. My reaction was: What can I write on worship that those with recognized world-class worship ministries have not already written or will not soon write? Many wonderful books have and will come forth, because this is the hour. Father God is drawing His people into deeper and higher worship—radical worship—all over the globe, to prepare the way to welcome His Son. There is increasing revelation and there are increasing depths and heights to which we can aspire.

I have at last come to accept that it was probably a true word. Here I am, writing a book on worship. I am writing this book not because of ultimately realizing that the word must have come from God; rather, I realize the word must have come from God because I finally find myself writing this book!

It is my intent simply to share what the Lord has taught through the experience of leading a small group of worshippers in Geneva, Switzerland. This initiative was born out of an ardent desire to worship Him non-stop, however ineptly at first, that gradually matured into effectual radical prophetic and intercessory worship.

Whom He appoints He anoints; and whom He calls, He equips. This means that if we have a burning desire, He will give us what we need to accomplish His purposes. Through this process, we learn more and more, because more and more is required of us.

So I invite you to share my journey and what we have learned along the way; and, as you do, may you be touched and enriched on your own journey. It is my heart's desire that, as you come along with me on this radical adventure, you will reap the blessings and share in the harvest. In this way, we can all go deeper and rise higher together in worship until all true worshippers meet the Lord in the air, as He comes for His spotless bride.

I

MY PERSONAL JOURNEY INTO RADICAL WORSHIP

B EFORE CONSIDERING THE "what," "when," "where," "why," and "how" of "breakthrough worship," allow me to lay one foundation stone here—that of my personal journey into intercessory worship. It is my hope that this might help you identify and relate your particular longings and experiences from your own heart of worship.

A. HIS "MASTERS" PROGRAM

At one point early in my career as an international lawyer, the Lord pulled me out of the market place for two years to pursue a "Master's degree" (Jesus being the "Master"), despite my having already earned a PhD. It appears He wanted me to dedicate focused time to truly learning of *Him*, before moving forward into what He was going to require of me in my God-ordained destiny.

Precisely two years from the beginning of His "Master's program," appropriately in the month of June, the Lord sovereignly confirmed my "Master's degree" with a one-word prophetic utterance at an intercessory prayer conference in the company of a multitude of believers, including my beloved pastor. I understood at once that the single word, "approved," delivered with the power of God through a trusted prophetic voice who knew nothing of my life or situation, was Father's express conferring of my "degree." I alone perceived the true meaning of this personal word—a word I have never shared until this moment, some thirty years later, not wanting it to be misinterpreted in any way that might suggest pride. I clearly understood it to relate purely to my "Master's degree." No more, no less. I in no way interpreted it to mean that I had "arrived."

In the course of this "Master's program," the Holy Spirit taught me many things experientially about living and walking by faith—not just believing but *acting on* His Word as if I truly believed it—things I had not grasped in a lifetime as a sincere, born-again, Bible-believing Christian.

Although this period was filled with amazing and precious "love tokens" from the Father, and brought me to a new level of spiritual sensitivity and communication with Him, it was not all a bed of roses. Much of it was heavy "boot camp" that, at times, made me cry out "how long, Lord; how long? Just help me learn the lessons You are trying to teach me so this can be over and we can move on!"

Putting on the whole armor of God

One very important lesson taught to me during this time by seasoned intercessors, who themselves had learned through painful experience, was to put on the whole armor of God daily, according to Ephesians 6:13–17, preferably with actual corresponding gestures, piece-by-piece. This is not just an exercise for novices; I still believe in putting on my armor daily, but especially before going into battle in intercession.

Some have responded to this practice with great self

assurance—that they see no need to repeat this daily, in that, once they had put on their armor, they had never taken it off. I wish I could share the same assurance, but I am not persuaded that my armor never slips. I figure that my armor can gap open—either asleep or awake. I reckon I can get a chink in my armor through an angry word or a prideful thought. I fear my armor can gap open should I fail to forgive my brother or should I hold resentment in my heart against an accuser or abuser.

What's more, were I to succeed in growing as I should, I might even require a bigger suit of armor fitted by God. I do not believe this is a matter of "one size fits all." I would like to suppose that I might grow in strength and stature and thereby be in need of a larger, stronger suit of armor.

But everyone should examine their own heart and hear God on this for themselves.

Growing by the Word and prayer

Among other disciplines adopted during this time set apart, I committed to reading five chapters of the Bible a day and to praying at least one hour a day. Although the prayer time sometimes extended well beyond an hour, the difficulty for me was *getting into* prayer, not *staying* in it for the duration (or often longer, once there). I needed to introduce some form of self-discipline, which at that time took the creative form of a commitment not to eat breakfast before having fulfilled my prayer time.

My "type A" (action-oriented) personality meant that on some days I might not eat breakfast until as late as 4:00 or so in the afternoon, by virtue of not having completed my prayer commitment any earlier. I must confess that there were occasional days where I failed altogether, for which I chastised myself, yet carried on the next day without using the failure as an excuse to slacken off.

Still, when the Lord spoke into my spirit to *double* my prayer time, I tried to reason with Him: "Father, can't we wait until I get the *one* hour really down right before we go to *two* hours?" Father's ears seemed to be stopped. He didn't argue; He just kept on repeating in my spirit: "Double your prayer time."

So, somewhat apprehensively, I tried doubling my prayer time to two hours. (*Caveat:* This was His word to me personally for that season, not to be taken as a universal requirement, any more than Jesus's word to the rich young ruler to go and sell all that he had necessarily compels all His would-be followers to do the same. We have only to be attentive to His word to us individually, wherever we are, for whatever season.)

"Praise Me"

After some months of these extended morning prayer times and five chapters of the Bible a day, I began to hear something else from the Spirit of God. I began to hear "Praise Me!" Well, I thought I *was* praising Him, so I respectfully but adamantly responded "Father, I *am* praising You!" Then I just carried on as before, possibly praising just a wee bit louder.

But when I *kept on hearing* "Praise Me," it finally got through to me that He was not satisfied. So, in an awkward but earnest attempt to increase my praise through physical expression and to thereby demonstrate to Him my sincerity, I started leaping while praising. Still, nothing seemed to change, and I *kept on* hearing "Praise Me"!

I can recall leaping and praising not only in my apartment in Washington DC, but also in a cabin in the woods of Pennsylvania where I hid away for a two-week self-appointed solitary retreat and first ever week-long fast, as a part of my seeking the Lord more diligently and delving more deeply into His ways. I still remember trying to leap high enough, with arms stretched heavenward, to reach the rafters of the cabin, like a small child saying "Daddy, see, I'm praising you!" But I felt nothing of His pleasure, and just went on hearing *"Praise Me!"*

One thing that has managed to get through my head over time, walking with Father, is that if you think you are obeying Him, yet He keeps on repeating the same thing that you think you are doing, heads up: *you are not doing it!*—at least not to His satisfaction.

I can remember still trying to chase this elusive quest when staying alone in the London apartment of a friend of a friend while there on some international law research.

I cannot really say when or how I actually arrived at praising Him more in line with the level of His expectations. I think there actually came a moment when I simply realized, somewhat to my surprise and distinct joy, that I was at last really praising Him freely and joyously with my whole being—body, soul, mind, and spirit. But it did not come from a fleshly effort; it emerged naturally from deep within. I knew I at last had the victory when the body language did not produce the praise; but the praise produced the body language.

At the same time, I cannot say that the physical demonstrations—out of a genuine sincerity and desire to obey and to please the Father—did not perhaps contribute to the ultimate positive outcome. These very acts may well have served to stimulate, in some measure, the depths of my being where my spirit dwells, and to some degree have helped to move me into that place of true and unfettered praise that Father and Son were asking of me.

The Father is moved even by our feeble and childlike attempts to draw closer to Him, however foolish these efforts may seem, just like an earthly father watching his precious child try, oh so awkwardly, to please daddy. Abba's heart, like daddy's, is touched and reaches out lovingly and tenderly, with pure delight, to His beloved child whose desire is to please Him.

B. The Victory

I cannot look back to a specific date on my calendar when I at last got the victory. While the realization came suddenly, the process was certainly a progressive one. All I know is that there are now virtually no restraints on my praise—at least if I am alone or with like-spirited worshippers who have their eyes only on the Beloved and not on anyone else in the room.

This still does not mean I have "arrived"; but the freedom and abandon have become a natural part and parcel of my worship, which in turn has totally changed, by virtue of pushing through to the higher praises. No longer do the stones have to "cry out" on my behalf; I can out-shout them any day or night!

> And when he was come nigh, even now at the descent of the mount of Olives, *the whole multitude of the disciples began to rejoice and praise God with a loud voice* for all the mighty works that they had seen; Saying, Blessed be the King that cometh in the name of the Lord: peace in heaven, and glory in the highest. And some of the Pharisees from among the multitude said unto him, Master, rebuke thy disciples.

And he answered and said unto them, I tell you
that, if these should hold their peace, the stones
would immediately cry out.

—LUKE 19:37–40, EMPHASIS ADDED

In some respects, it is much the same with worship as
with praise. For me personally, the deeper worship followed on from the higher praise, over the course of time.
I have similarly found that, in an abbreviated time frame,
over the course of a single evening, the high praise attracts
His awesome presence which, in turn, ushers in the worship. This is because, as promised, He comes and dwells in
the midst of our praises.

Therefore with joy shall ye draw water out of the
wells of salvation.

And in that day shall ye say, *Praise the Lord*,
call upon his name, declare his doings among the
people, make mention that his name is exalted. *Sing
unto the Lord*; for he hath done excellent things: this
is known in all the earth. *Cry out and shout*, thou
inhabitant of Zion: *for great is the Holy One of Israel
in the midst of thee.*

—ISAIAH 12:3–6, EMPHASIS ADDED

C. SUMMING UP

Thus my "Master's Program" was a life-changing and critical preparation for my future Christian walk and prayer
life—a definite spiritual turning point. All along the way
were extraordinary confirmations and milestones, as
well as those precious surprise "love tokens" that prove
to us that, even as His eye is on the sparrow, He cares
for the smallest aspect of our lives. It is often these most
intimate and personalized details that demonstrate to us,

even more than the greater miracles, the deeply personal nature of His love and care. The sum total of both served to encourage me that, yes, this "time-out" was indeed ordained by Him, the ultimate and supreme *Master.*

Each of you will have your own experience and your own pathway to the throne, but I will end this personal note by adding that, in a lifetime of walking with the Lord (I loved Jesus as early as I can remember—as early as I knew His name), nothing has so utterly changed my spiritual life as worship—*nothing!* Worship night is still my most anticipated night of the week.

II

FORMING A LOCAL WORSHIP GROUP—A PERSONAL EXPERIENCE

A. How It All Began

My own journey into corporate prophetic worship all started in Geneva. While working for the United Nations in that strategic place, I helped found an international church, "Church for the Nations," where I served, *inter alia*, as an elder and as a member of the ministry/prayer team. We often experienced beautiful and anointed worship which, over time, was extended to about an hour at the start of the Sunday morning service. I was also a part of the revolving worship team—at times leading—yet my spirit and soul were not satisfied.

The heart's desire

On the "best" Sundays, when the praise and worship would really usher in the manifest presence of God, it was often interrupted at its height—to take the offering, to share the announcements, to add a word from the pulpit, or to actually move on to the message—while my spirit was still in the flow of worship and longed to continue in that realm.

I still recall one Sunday morning in which our worship

leader had brought us right to the door of the throne room, on the very verge of entering into the glory. But just as we were at the threshold, the pastor took over the microphone—for whatever reason—and we were all arrested at the door. By the time he turned the microphone back over to the worship leader, the glory had departed. I remember in particular that the next worship song was expressly about "the glory," but the glory would not return on cue, and we did not go through the door.

This incident only deepened my desire for unbroken worship and further nurtured my vision to one day have an entire evening each week where we could just go on worshipping and worshipping without interruption, free to enter into the glory zone and then to stay there!

Realizing the desire

It would be a number of years before this burning desire of my heart for a regular night where *nothing* would disturb the worship was to become a reality. And when it did, it was not by the planning of man. It all began with a phone call from a precious woman lawyer intercessor in London whom I had met there some six months prior at a prayer-for-the-nations conference. She related to me how their small prayer group felt led to hold an all-night prayer meeting for Geneva, having obeyed the same prompting with regard to Brussels the month before. The purpose of her call was to ask if I had any special insights to guide their intercession for Geneva, where I had already lived for some ten years at that time.

I gladly and gratefully embraced her initiative and offered to pull together a group of the willing from my church to pray all night, along with them, forming a sort of "bridge" or "rainbow" of prayer, with London at one end and Geneva at the other.

I knew Father was in it from the start, but one clear token of His divine involvement emerged only after I learned the scheduling for the London side of the event. I was informed in due course that the London group would be meeting to pray from 8 p.m. to 5 a.m. This struck me as a bit odd, since it did not seem to coincide with any of the normal night watches (e.g., 6–9 p.m., 9–12 p.m., 12–3 a.m., 3–6 a.m.).

Then one day it suddenly dawned on me that 8 p.m. to 5 a.m. in London would be 9 p.m. to 6 a.m. in Geneva—the very hours we had arranged to pray that night! We had not planned the timing together to coincide in this way. Nor, I later learned, were the hours of the London vigil set for any reason at all related to the different time zones. They were arranged to accommodate certain work schedules of would-be participants. This precise orchestration had the Father's fingerprints all over it. He had sovereignly set up the perfect coordination for a synchronized night-watch for Geneva, initiated in London, on Geneva time! What care and precision! What confirmation!

Supposing this to be a one-time event for us in Geneva, and hardly knowing where we were going or how we were to get there, we were determined to praise and pray for Geneva—and the many nations with diplomatic representation there—all night long.

We had no worship team to lead us or even any form of live music at all to inspire us. So we did a lot of spontaneous singing and group dancing to keep ourselves alert and awake, to stay on focus, and to keep in unity.

Even that first night, in our impromptu—if not to say somewhat awkward—circle dancing, scarcely knowing what we were doing, we instinctively called out nations and snatched them out of the fire prophetically in our dance. We also joined in victory marches and other intercessory prophetic acts throughout the night, though it did not so much as enter my mind to associate such intercession with worship.

By morning, when the pastor and pastor's wife came looking for a bedraggled, beleaguered, bleary-eyed remnant, they arrived to find a full contingent of wide-eyed, animated women (we were all women that first night). Indeed, we were so exhilarated from the experience that, by 6 a.m., those present were asking if I would lead such all-night prayer every week or every other week. I suggested starting out with once a month, and that's how we began our adventure in all-night intercessory worship for Geneva, Switzerland, Israel, and the nations.

I did not recognize at the outset that this was my worship-night vision coming into fulfillment. I thought of it simply as "all-night prayer for Geneva, Israel, and the nations," although I never moved into intercession without first entering into praise and worship to seek the heart of the Father.

My own primary aspiration—whether in individual or in corporate worship—is to *enter in* to His presence and come close enough and linger long enough to hear His heart. Only from that place can we truly intercede for His purposes. My aim has always been to *avoid* praying our opinions; indeed, we should avoid praying *at all* until we have reached the throne of God and gotten in touch with *His* heart. Only then can we effectively pray His plans and His will for the nations.

How do we get to the throne to hear His heart? Through

worship. I had only the promise that the Holy Spirit will guide us into worship "in spirit and in truth."

> But the hour cometh, and now is, when the true worshippers shall worship the Father in spirit and in truth: for the Father seeketh such to worship him. God is a Spirit: and they that worship him must worship him in spirit and in truth.
>
> —JOHN 4:23–24

So worship is how we always began our all-night prayer gatherings. Still, I did not think of the worship itself as intercession.

As we continued to meet to intercede all night for the nations, the Holy Spirit led us more and more into praise and worship *as* intercession, rather than praise and worship *and* intercession. Indeed, we came to find praise and worship to be one of the highest and most effectual forms of intercession.

We interceded in singing—in the Spirit and in familiar songs, backed up by selected anointed CDs in the absence of live music; we interceded in spontaneous group dancing and "victory" marches—drawing us into greater unity and increased joyfulness and strength for the battle; we interceded with banners—small ones to begin with, and later, much larger ones, already in anticipation of an eventual permanent house of "24/7" worship and prayer in or near Geneva.

I had not imagined that these related streams of prayer and praise would merge and evolve into something I would come to know as "harp and bowl" ministry and "intercessory worship." I was not even familiar with those terms at that time. In fact, the first time I came across the term "harp and bowl," in a Christian magazine, I was so excited that I exclaimed out loud, alone in my living room: "That's it! That's what we do!" I searched the Scriptures for the origin of this concept and found it in the Book of Revelation:

> And when he had taken the book, the four beasts and four and twenty elders fell down before the Lamb, having every one of them *harps, and golden vials [bowls]* full of odours, *which are the prayers of saints.*
>
> —REVELATION 5:8, EMPHASIS ADDED

"*Harps*" and "*bowls*" —*music* combined with *intercession*—the prayers of the saints carried upward on the music! I at once determined I would one day go to one of Mike Bickle's "harp and bowl" conferences to learn more. This I eventually did, to my further enrichment and benefit.

The ministry

On these worship nights, as a rule, we do not engage in personal prophecy or individual prayer. Any personal ministry for a special need, if at all, is normally held for the end. I am most certainly in favor of personal prayer and prophecy, but there are many other times and places appropriate for—and geared toward—individual ministry. My desire was and is to have *just one regular night* where we would focus wholly and exclusively on *Him*, honoring only *Him* and seeking nothing for ourselves.

My sense is that, because Father blesses us over and over again, many times and in many ways, we should be willing to set apart one night in seven where our sole object is to bless *Him*—to gather to lift Him up, to adore Him, to tell Him He is worthy, to tell Him He is mighty, to pour out our love and adoration upon Him—in a word, to minister unto *Him* alone.

The outcome for our particular group in Geneva was that, in some unprogrammed progression, without man's planning or aforethought, the Holy Spirit gradually brought us to a level of worship that could serve as intercession to fill the bowls in heaven. The substance of our worship could then, in turn, be poured out over the nations—represented in that place by the United Nations and the many national diplomatic missions established there—wherever the Father saw the greatest or most appropriate need on any given night.

The "all-night prayer" for Geneva, Israel, and the nations thereby turned into nights of "intercessory worship" unto God, the Father and the Son, by the Holy Spirit, for the Godhead to use as "prayer substance," at His discretion. The objective remained the same, only reinforced with more power—our worship filling the bowls to be poured out according to the Father's all-knowing eye over the nations, and our warfare worship reaching wherever He knew to be the neediest. Verbal prayers and declarations are also pronounced, as the Spirit gives utterance, out of the midst of the worship.

You do not need to be in Geneva to reach the nations! You just need a desire that He give you the nations—or your city, or your neighborhood—as your inheritance! You fill the bowls by your worship; He distributes to the uttermost parts of the earth. You inherit the fruits.

> Ask of me, and I shall give thee the heathen [Gentiles/ nations] for thine inheritance, and the uttermost parts of the earth for thy possession.
>
> —PSALM 2:8

God is simply looking for those who will worship Him "in spirit and in truth." Of course we cannot help but receive a blessing in return as we worship, simply by experiencing His pleasure at our desire to fellowship with Him and by abiding in His presence. But "receiving" is not our objective; our objective is rather to give, to pour out, unto our worthy and magnificent Maker and Savior and King!

Summing up

So this is how our worship became seamlessly blended into our intercession and how our intercession became seamlessly blended into our worship—"harp and bowl" intercessory worship. The worship *became* intercession and the intercession *became* worship which, upon reaching the heart of the Father, was returned in love, filling, in turn, the heart of the worshipper to align with and accomplish His divine purposes.

And that's how, for us, it all began.

B. How It All Evolved

I don't want to overemphasize Geneva, but it is this experience that has taught me nearly everything I know about intercessory worship and therefore serves as my personal point of reference. It is precisely what I have learned through this awesome assignment that I can hope to pass on to others.

The rest of the story is a progressive one, learning to perceive the difference between "active" and "passive" worship, learning what pleased and what displeased the Holy Spirit, learning what disturbed the atmosphere of prayer, learning what brought down or raised the anointing/ Presence, learning how to sustain worship, learning how to move corporately, learning how to stay in the flow, learning…learning…learning…We are still—and will forever be—learning. The Holy Spirit is the teacher *par excellence*, and there will always be more to learn.

It is not my intent to drag the reader through that whole process here, but rather to share the final fruits of what we have gleaned, up to the present time.

After about five years of monthly all-night prayer, we began to desire more frequent worship nights, even if not all night, while still holding all-night prayer once a month. So we began a weekly worship night as well, which I called "Breakthrough Worship." At first I put out a small e-mail notice announcing "worship from 7:00 to 9:00." But we found we weren't ready to stop at 9:00. So the next week I changed it to "7:00 to 9:30." Same outcome: we could not stop worshipping. So the following week my announcement read "7:00–10:30," but even then we had a hard time closing. No one wanted to leave His awesome presence; we would linger on in the afterglow, often prostrate on the floor, while the "closing out" instrumental (the same every week) played on. So, in the end, I simply announced: "Breakthrough Worship—7:00 p.m."

I soon discovered, with our willingness to adapt, that the Holy Spirit—if we allowed Him the freedom—seemed to want about three hours of our worship. When we moved the starting time up to 8 p.m. to accommodate certain schedules, I could virtually start up worship at 8 o'clock, never look at my watch, and when I sensed the Holy Spirit was satisfied and preparing to close, only then look at the time and find it to be right around 11:00 p.m. This happened so consistently that, henceforward, any time we changed the starting time, we maintained this three-hour time frame. We have since moved to 9 p.m., but the duration of three hours still holds—9 to 12 midnight. At midnight, twelve bells ring out in the clear mountain air from our little 700–year–old village church. It seems a fitting close.

(*Caveat*: Do not be put off by any impression that there is an all-night or a three-hour standard that must be met in order not to grieve the Holy Spirit. Remember, this is not a "one size fits all." Seek the Lord for your particular group and circumstances. You might wish to start with an hour and see what God does. Just be sensitive and He will show you His pleasure for your unique assignment.)

C. How We Got Here

So how did we end up worshipping in a 700–year–old village church on the side of the Jura mountains overlooking Geneva? Well, for that I have to come back and fill in a bit on those five years, as regards the *"physical"* journey that accompanied the *spiritual* one.

Seeking His "special place"

Our Geneva all-night worship began, quite naturally, in the Church for the Nations, of which I was a founder/member. But after some time, I began to hear persistently in my spirit: "It's bigger than these four walls." This I did not interpret to mean a greater *size* but rather a greater *scope*—more "apostolic"—a more neutral ground where others, beyond just one church, would feel comfortable. But were we ready to lengthen our cords and strengthen our stakes and increase the place of our habitation (see Isaiah 54:2)? Were we ready to move out beyond our comfort zone?

Confirmation through open doors

I recall over twenty years ago, in Washington DC, a woman of God said that any new ministry needs to be "confirmed" by God. For some reason, that has always stayed with me. Did God really care about this small worship "ministry" in the bowels of Geneva? Could it indeed be deemed a "ministry" at all? We know He loves to receive our worship, and we know we love to render our worship unto Him; but is this a "ministry" truly ordained of Him? Will He confirm it?

All I could hear was, "It's bigger than these four walls," and on that basis I began my search for a place of Father's choosing. I must have visited virtually every church on Geneva's "Right Bank" (the north side of the Lake)—churches of every denomination, including Roman Catholic and Greek Orthodox, and, when actually making personal contact, explaining my mission and guardedly casting my eyes upward to check for high ceilings! We needed space to move and dance before the Lord, and we needed high ceilings to accommodate our worship banners. But we also needed an open door.

"Special Place" #1

God led us to that open door in a pretty little Swiss chapel with soft yellow exterior, tucked away in the trees like a tiny refuge in Geneva's "seedy nightlife" district, east of the central train station. This "special place" was in Father's sovereign plan and provision, and so He gave us favor and, literally, the key—an open door. *Confirmation.*

It was ideally suited to our needs and desires, with a leadership that was in tune with our prophetic intercessory vision. Stackable chairs afforded the space we sought for freedom of movement, and the ceilings were just right for raising high our flags and banners! We gratefully established ourselves here to carry on our monthly all-night intercession, which continued to take place on Friday nights so that we could sleep in on Saturday mornings.

This little church periodically held an extended school of prophecy on one Saturday per month. It so happened that one month the school fell on the Saturday following our all-night prayer. A few days later, I received a call from the pastor, requesting that we schedule our monthly gatherings to regularly coincide with his monthly prophecy course. He explained that the presence of God had been so strong when they arrived on that Saturday morning that the anointing on the day's teaching was notably enhanced. We of course were greatly blessed by this report and joyfully agreed to coordinate with their schedule. *Confirmation.*

After about two years, the church's own scheduling changed and it was the Father's time to strategically move us on. Thus the search for location began again and nothing was ruled out that might provide space to move freely and high ceilings for our banners…and an open door.

"Special Place" #2

As the new search got underway, I began to hear in my spirit: "the gates," which was spontaneously reinforced from various external sources. Then one day I happened onto a beautiful 400-year-old stone chapel, hidden away on a back road just off and behind the motorway entering Geneva—thus at the very "gates" of the city.

Not only is the motorway, at that point, the only route along the Lake into Geneva, but also just a few yards from the back of the chapel run the only railroad tracks into Geneva. So every car on the Lake route and every train arriving into Geneva has to pass by that entry point—that "gate" into the city.

Why Father didn't lead me there at once, only He knows. But there is a time and a season for every purpose under heaven, and God's timing is always perfect!

> To every thing there is a season, and a time to every
> purpose under the heaven.
>
> —ECCLESIASTES 3:1

While still seeking out the appropriate persons for enquiry into its possible use for our weekly worship, yet nonetheless ever in search of a "high place" (the chapel being at lake level), I one day pulled into the drive of a stately home at a high point overlooking the Lake of Geneva that I had been eyeing for some time for possible use of the *"orangerie"* for our worship. (An *"orangerie"* is a large outdoor greenhouse where orange trees are grown, traditionally on large estates or royal grounds. This would give us a large empty space and a high glass ceiling!) I had, up to then, never found anyone home, and, once again, no one answered at the grand front entrance. But just as I was leaving, a car pulled in to the circular drive and out stepped what turned out to be the heiress of the (uninhabited) house. (Did I say God's timing is always perfect?)

In sharing with her my quest, she revealed that her father had been the pastor of the little old stone church that I had just discovered at the "gates," which, indeed, was straight down the hill from her house, as the crow flies. She reminisced about running up and down that hill through the wildflowers as a child, between her family home and her father's chapel. He had since been promoted to heaven.

She offered us the use of her unoccupied but still-furnished family home for our worship meeting (the orangery being unsuitable for immediate use) and received us there on the appointed evening in a bright red dress, sharing something of her life and family with us for a while and then leaving us to our worship. It was an awesome and memorable journey into faded glory—this stately home reeking with time-worn elegance and local history, with a direct historical and personal link to the chapel at the "gates"! After beginning our prayer time indoors, we moved outdoors to pray around the grounds and over the fields sweeping down to the old stone chapel below.

We did not feel led to hold further meetings at the stately home, but I believe we were claiming the territory that night—from the higher heights on down to the little stone chapel, where, in God's own time, we were destined to make our more lasting footprint, at the "gates."

In the days that followed, upon meeting with the pastor overseeing this parish, I learned that services are seldom held in this particular one of three "sister" chapels of the parish, owing to the noise of the frequently passing trains, and that, for this reason, it is rarely used, other than for weddings. For us, a passing train would be a great opportunity for a collective shout! No problem for us! And in the Father's perfect provision, the old wooden pews could be pushed back to create space, and the wooden vaulted ceilings were more than high enough for our flags and banners!

The pastor graciously and readily agreed to open up this precious "wedding" chapel for our regular nights of intercessory worship. Once more, by God's divine favor, I was entrusted with the key. As a "foreigner" and—just as with "special place" #1—an "outsider" to the parish, this was received as from the Father's hand. When God chooses the "special place," He gives you favor…and the key! Another open door. *Confirmation.*

Later I was even to discover that this was the very pastor who conducted the marriage of my Swiss neighbors who would become the parents of my Swiss godchild.

God chose this "special place" for this special baby to later be dedicated to God by myself, in the presence—and with the additional blessings—of our worship group. God is full of surprises and love-token confirmations.

Thus the "special place" chosen by God for our new strategic assignment was the little stone chapel at the very "gates" of Geneva—Geneva, known as the "City of God" and the political "seat" of the nations. He has a "special place" for every assignment, and you will know when you have found it. He will *confirm* it.

Speaking of *confirmation*, at one time I lost the use of my car for several months. How would I get down the mountain from my home to the little back road of the chapel for Breakthrough Worship nights with no transportation available—private or public? The only possibility was to trundle all my equipment down to my tiny village train station, take the little red and orange train down the mountain, change to another all-local-stops train along the Lake to the last stop before the central Geneva train station, then proceed some fifteen to twenty minutes by foot from the tiny local train stop to the chapel. This, in winter, with all the musical equipment, banners, flags of nations, and the rest, was virtually impossible.

We would sorely miss not having our worship meetings—the best night of the week! But did *Father* really care whether or not we met together during this problematic interval? After all, we could each worship Him in our respective homes over this time, could we not? Surely He would understand.

I was soon to learn, however, how important this intercessory worship meeting was not only to us but also to Father God, and that He expects us to keep guard in the strategic places where He has set us as watchmen on the wall. And just watch! It is He who makes a way where there is no way! Heads up: He cares!

In a word, Father amazingly and sovereignly sent "unique" and totally unanticipated "chariots" each week, engaging some near stranger or other, for some spontaneous and extraordinary reason, literally to come up the mountain and take me down to the chapel at the "gates," with all my equipment. None of my "benefactors" were in any way aware of my plight or circumstances beforehand, but Father supplied a different solution on each and every one of those Breakthrough Worship nights for as long as I was without transportation.

After about six weeks of such clearly divine provision, we decided to meet the next week in the little church up in my village on the mountainside, a stone's throw away from my house. I could easily make it there on foot within minutes of my doorstep, without the need of a special "chariot."

That night it seemed like a real "push through" against stubborn spiritual resistance, as if we were ploughing new ground, and I realized how easy it had become to break through in the little chapel at the "gates." Our worship had, it seems, over the several years we were there, opened the heavens over that and the surrounding area. In fact, one night not long before, we had emerged from our Breakthrough Worship to discover unusual light in the sky all around, for which we could identify no natural source. We all gazed at this phenomenon, each one silently daring to consider whether it could be a supernatural sign of breakthrough over this strategic gateway to Geneva.

We will only know when we get to heaven, but in retrospect it would appear that, if it truly was a sign from heaven, the message was that the time had come for us to move on to the next "special place." It was very soon afterward that we found ourselves up the mountain, though we did not know at the time that we were sovereignly being relocated there indefinitely, as "special place" #3.

"Special Place" #3

Our provisional change of venue just "happened" to fall immediately after the weekend celebration of the 700th anniversary of this little village church on the side of the Jura mountains. Historically, it is an offshoot of the very first monastery in all of Switzerland,* whose ruins still exist today above the village. We felt that holding our Breakthrough Worship there that night was planned by Father as a "private" yet integral part of the commemoration. We had a sense of re-digging the wells and reviving the ancient prayers that had once arisen over centuries from this "special place."

At the end of that "one-off" night of pressing through, we all expressed the sense that our mission was not finished there and that we should return there the following week. After the second week, we felt we needed to return yet a third time. A few days later, I received a letter from the parish church board of the chapel at the "gates," telling us graciously that they were closing its doors to us for the rest of the winter, owing to heating costs and other upkeep issues, but that we were welcome to return in the spring. Clearly, Father had planned well ahead for this transition and had already transplanted us from the "gates" literally to the "heights," even before that door was closed. What prearrangement! What *confirmation* of His care and infinitely detailed involvement!

---

* The *chartreuse Notre-Dame d'Oujon*, founded in AD 1146.

And so it was that Father placed us first at the very heart of Geneva, then moved us to its "gates," and then on up to the "heights" above it, all the while taking care to see that there was never an interruption in the Breakthrough Worship—*confirmation* that God cared intensely about these weekly gatherings to honor Him and to seek His heart in worship. He had positioned us strategically to break through for Geneva, Israel, and the nations, and it was in His interest that we keep our engagement with Him, in whatever place He had appointed, without fail!

Confirmation through financial provision

One final word on *confirmation*. Father often confirms a ministry assignment by financial provision. In our case, we needed no resources where we first began, in our own church; thus no test. The same was true of "special place" #1, which welcomed us with no monetary conditions.

"Special place" #2, on the other hand, required a weekly set "donation" that was not inconsiderable, to cover heating and other costs and inconveniences of the chapel's upkeep. No offering was ever asked of the worshippers, but between spontaneous freewill offerings and, ultimately, consecutive long-term monthly pledges from current and former worshippers, we always had just enough to meet our obligations.

In the Father's characteristic timing and precision, it was just as the generous pledges came to an end from our worshippers who had by then left the Geneva area for other postings, that we were moving on to "special place" #3, my village church. Despite the well running dry, by faith we offered to contribute for at least our use of the heating and lighting. The dear Swiss pastor's response was that he was simply happy to have the church in use and that we were welcome to avail ourselves of it freely, with his blessing.

We still have a balance of thirty-three centimes in our account *"Ministère,"* the same amount we had upon arrival at my village church. His provision is always enough and never too much, in order to keep us aware that it is God who is our Provider and who confirms His work in many ways, not the least of which, through His exact provision.

Summing up

We are still meeting on the "heights." We never went back down the mountain. The view from my village on the side of the Jura extends all the way up the Lake of Geneva, past the *"gates,"* to the famous *jet d'eau* at the *heart* of Geneva. This is a landmark fountain jetting high into the sky out of Lac Léman (the "Lake of Geneva"). We can literally see back along all the way that we have come, with a sense that He has lengthened our cords, strengthened our stakes, and enlarged the place of our habitation.

> Enlarge the place of thy tent, and let them stretch forth the curtains of thine habitations: spare not, lengthen thy cords, and strengthen thy stakes; For thou shalt break forth on the right hand and on the left; and thy seed shall inherit the Gentiles, and make the desolate cities to be inhabited.
>
> —ISAIAH 54:2–3

We are prepared to move forward to "special place" #4, if and whenever He so ordains. But until then, we will "stay with the cloud." We simply want to be available and obedient, as we are passionately desirous of the nations ("Gentiles") as our inheritance. You too will He plant strategically, according to your particular calling, if you wait upon Him to lead you to His "special place." Rest assured that, as you "follow the cloud," even as God led His people in the wilderness, He will be faithful to watch over your express assignment to perform it.

III

ACTIVE VS. PASSIVE WORSHIP

ONCE MORE, BEFORE moving on to the "what," "when," "where," "why," and "how" of breakthrough worship, I would like to share an observation from our Geneva experience that led me to draw a distinction between "active" and "passive" worship.

Please do not misunderstand me. *All* worship is good. But I learned through our all-night worship in Geneva that there is a difference between what I would call "active" as compared to "passive" worship, and I want to pass that on to you here.

A. PASSIVE WORSHIP

"Passive worship" I would describe as coming into the presence of the Lord and receiving from Him as you partake of a Spirit-filled atmosphere created by anointed music or by worship and/or intercession in which you may not have actively participated.

If you are particularly in need of spiritual refreshing, restoration, or inner healing, it is truly a blessing to be able to drink in such an atmosphere of heaven brought down by other worshippers. Everything from God is good.

His very presence is good. So we can come in and simply receive.

"Soaking"

This leads quite naturally to the subject of "soaking." "Soaking" is normally understood to mean simply being still—often prone—and passively absorbing the presence of the Lord from soft anointed music—live or recorded. Such passive worship can refresh the soul and serve to increase intimacy with Father and Son, by the Holy Spirit.

It is always rewarding to take time to wait upon the Lord and to commune one-on-one with Him. This *passive* "soaking" can be a great source of comfort if you are simply in need of rest and restoration, a deep healing touch, or just a quiet and concentrated time of sweet communion. This is the Lord ministering to us.

"Soaking" is not *always passive* worship. We may have *actively* participated in bringing in the atmosphere of heaven—for example, over the course of a night of breakthrough worship, where, at the end, we simply want to linger and soak in the afterglow and go on drinking in His awesome presence. This too can be a beautiful time of deep communion and rest from the spiritual battles often waged during intercessory praise and worship. Although we will often have experienced great joy and His mighty arm of strength in the midst of the battle, when it is done, we gladly let the Spirit of God minister unto us, in His turn.

Whether by virtue of *active* worshippers already worshipping or interceding in the room—often with the support of anointed psalmists or through perhaps no more than an anointed CD—it should be noted that *someone* has had to *actively* bring down the Presence that you are now *passively* enjoying. Even with anointed CDs, the singers themselves will have at some previous point taken time to come *actively* into the Presence that is now flowing out through that music into your spirit, as you *passively* receive.

The benefits of moving from "passive" to "active" worship

If you or others have not already participated in the *active* worship and/or intercession in that place, that Presence which you are *passively* enjoying might well not be there to touch you so profoundly. While this *passive* worship is comforting and oh so good, if you are really in need of refreshing, you will be blessed to learn that you can receive an even deeper touch if in fact you have managed to enter in to the *active* worship that has served to usher in God's restorative anointing. The refreshing waters will then be flowing from the inside out rather than from the outside in.

When you *actively* participate in calling in the Holy Spirit and inviting the worshipping angels, and do not leave to the worship leaders and other *active* worshippers the full responsibility of drawing down the angels from heaven to touch the earth, and the sole onus of pulling in the anointing, you yourself will enter into the heavenly realms more readily, and thereby be all the more impacted personally by His Spirit. This is particularly true in a small group, where each worshipper plays a greater proportional role.

You may sometimes feel like all you have the strength to do is to sit with head in hands or resting on your arms on the the pew in front of you and soak in the refreshing of His presence drawn down by the other worshippers.

Father will mercifully meet you where you are and bless and restore and minister to you and encircle you in His everlasting arms. Such is good, and at times necessary. But, for the intercessor, this should not become habitual, and it should not be mistaken for intercession. Intercession for cities and nations is often a battlefield and is not the place for tired or wounded warriors. For that we must be prepared to enter in to *active*—if not *radical*—worship, if we are to rise to the level of breakthrough.

It should be noted here that it is our own spiritual state that often determines the level of anointing reached in our worship. We must avoid placing the entire responsibility on the worship leaders if the anointing seems to be weak or singularly uninspiring on a particular occasion, or (dare I say) judging them when you are not personally lifted higher. Sometimes we need to search our own hearts. We may find we are in unforgiveness, bitterness, pride, or some other subtle sin that is hindering the working of the Holy Spirit in us. We may be in need of repentance. If so, delay no longer. Repent and join in to *active* worship!

B. Active Worship

In *active* worship, you will want to run to meet the Bridegroom, to shout to Him, to call His name, to cry out to your Beloved, to draw down His presence by fully engaging with Him. You may sing in the Spirit; you may blow the shofar (by the Spirit please!). You will inject energy and passion into your worship. It would appear that He loves that, because when He hears it for three hours every Sunday night on the mountainside outside and overlooking Geneva, He comes—every time.

In fact, you will find—if you keep your "special place"

sanctified—that as you enter that place on your worship night, you will sense the presence of angels already gathered there, expectantly waiting. And then, as you enter in *actively*, He comes—Father, Son, Holy Spirit. He comes. You become filled with Him, and His life source and Holy Ghost boldness are transmitted to you. You are ready to make holy proclamations and to "prophesy to the wind" (Ezek. 37:9)—intercession empowered by His Spirit. And as you worship Him to the point of "breakthrough," you will feel His Spirit well up within you, and you will be ready to do exploits in His name, by the power of His might!

That may mean being a little "radical"; that may mean being a little "violent," but it is written: *"The violent take it by force"* (see Matthew 11:12). The walls of Jericho fell by the loud shouts and shofars of the people and priests (see Joshua 6:1–20); and if *we* do not cry out, the very *stones* will cry *out!* (see Luke 19:40). He *wants* us to cry *out.* The harder the territory He gives us, the more "work" we may have in order to *break through*.

It is somehow hard to imagine *breaking through* softly, passively. There are times for His gentleness, and it is wonderful for you personally; but this is not likely to provide the *breakthrough* you will need in intercession for cities and nations. Moreover, as noted above, if you approach this intercession passively, you are far less likely to fully break through even for yourself.

Personal breakthrough

I always refrain from interfering in someone's personal style of worship. I am glad to have any sincere worshipper's presence and faithful participation. But I perceive in some worshippers a real need to shout aloud, to release the flow not only for effectual intercession but first and foremost for their own spiritual breakthrough. The Lord says, *"open your mouth wide, and I will fill it"*! (See Psalm 81:10.) So we need to open our mouth wide, and when He fills it, He then wants us to *do* something with that filling. Intercession!

It's not *just* for your city; a beneficial byproduct is that it brings breakthrough for *you* as well! You become a vessel for God's power, for His anointing. Nothing will be impossible unto you, because the Holy Spirit is in you and overflows out of you to accomplish God's purposes on the earth. You yourself will be strengthened by the power of *His* might! Then you can go forth and do exploits!

What does the Word of God say? It says that the Lord inhabits the praises of His people (see Psalm 22:3). So we tend to think of that in general terms: when we praise, the Lord inhabits our praises—as a gathering of His people. This is glorious, corporately speaking. But the good news is that it is the *same for you personally*, individually speaking! When *you* praise, He inhabits *your* praises, and *you* experience breakthrough! Then that in turn gives you more power to break through for your city and your country—for the nations! Effectual intercession!

Loud versus quiet worship

Please understand that I do not mean that all quiet worship is necessarily "passive" and that all "active" worship is necessarily loud. But remember that the subject here is intercessory worship. One seasoned intercessor has defined "to intercede" as: "to open the mouth and to release the breath of God forcefully." For *intercession*—especially for nations, cities, and other territorial landmarks—the worship needs at times to be not only *active* but even *explosive*. Declarations may need to be pronounced boldly for the bringing down of strongholds. Prophecy from the throne room may need to be released dynamically into the earth. There are no strict rules, other than to follow the leading of the Holy Spirit. Speak what He speaks; go where He goes.

You may actually be surprised, at times, where He leads you. For example, even when you have *broken through* in praise and *active* worship, you may find yourself next being led into a garden of delight, for lighthearted frolicking and refreshing. Or He may choose to lead you into His very chambers, where you may find yourself unable to so much as open your mouth to speak, or where you feel you can scarcely breathe. You may be so at one with Him that you dare not—cannot—break the silence, even to praise Him—devoid of words, motionless, "frozen," as it were, in time and space. Now, *that*, even though breathlessly still, is *not* passive worship. Such worship, though essentially "quiet," is *active* and powerful to deliver.

In a word, "active"/"passive" has nothing to do with loud/quiet. It has to do with the state of your spirit and even your will to enter in unreservedly. It depends on *your* spirit connecting with the *Holy* Spirit. You can be prone on the floor, "lifeless," motionless, and yet be in intensely *active* worship.

Summing up

To sum up, then: *passive* worship is basically God ministering to us; *active* worship is essentially us ministering to God. Both are good. But for *intercession*, the real intercessory and prophetic *power* comes through *active* worship, in which we become totally involved—with our voice, with our body, with our mind, with our soul, and above all, with our spirit, connecting with His Spirit for *breakthrough*.

IV

BREAKTHROUGH WORSHIP

So WHAT ABOUT "breakthrough worship"? Let's at last turn together to the questions of "*what* is worship?," "*why* do we worship?," "*whom* do we worship?," "*when* do we worship?," "*where* do we worship?," "*how* do we worship?," "*with whom* do we worship?," and "*with what* do we worship?"

A. WHAT IS WORSHIP?

When I first asked the dear Swiss pastor in my mountain village if we could use the village church for our weekly three-hour worship, his response was: "You're going to sit in silence for three hours?" This was his concept of worship: silence.

Not only is worship *not* just silently waiting upon God, but *neither* is it even primarily silent. Worship is actively reaching out toward Him. It is not holding out our hands to receive—even a spiritual blessing—but rather stretching them upward toward Him, to bless Him, to honor Him, to acknowledge who He is, and to tell Him how we feel about Him—how great and magnificent He is, how much we love Him, and how thankful we are that He first loved us. It is all about *Him.* So we are not limited to waiting upon Him; we can rush headlong to fall before His throne—to cast our crowns at His feet and to call out His wonderful name(s)!

So to consider "WHAT is worship," let us begin with what worship is *not*.

What worship is not

In America, we normally call a Sunday morning church service—or essentially any organized church gathering where hymns are sung and a sermon is preached—a "worship service." While such a service may be spiritually instructive and even inspirational, it should not be characterized as a "worship" service in the biblical sense of the word—where the sole object is *worshipping* the Almighty.

In the typical Sunday morning "worship service," Christians get together, which is good; they sing a few hymns together, which is good; they hear a message together, which is (hopefully) good; and they recite prayers together, which is good. But is this really a *worship* service? Is there a special dedicated time truly set aside to prepare our hearts to enter into the holy place, to look into His face, to adore Him with our hearts and our lips, singing praises to His holy name and losing ourselves in Him, giving honor to His holy presence?

While we may all agree that worship is not merely keeping silence, neither is it simply voicing spiritual words. Worship does not consist in just the singing of spiritual hymns and traditional or modern Christian songs. Even if we utter or sing the words, "Father, we worship You," "Jesus, we adore You," "Father, we praise You," Jesus, we love You," this in itself does not constitute worship. It is not in the *saying* or in the *singing*; it is not even in the *doing*; it is in the "*being*." "*Lord, make me an instrument of worship!*"

What worship should be

So what *is* worship? Worship is the unreserved pouring out of our love and adoration to the Father and the Son, with the help of the Holy Spirit. To worship is to bow down, body and soul, before the King of the universe, the Savior of the world, in awe, in respect, and in all humility. To worship is to give God honor, to give God glory, to give God thanks, to give God praise, to tell Him how wonderful He is, to tell Him how much we love Him and that He is altogether worthy forever to be praised and adored.

> Give unto the LORD the glory due unto his name;
> worship the LORD in the beauty of holiness.
> —PSALM 29:2

To worship is to please *Him*—to bless *Him!* To worship is to sing *to* Him, not *about* Him (a "revelation" taught to me naturally by the Spirit of God in the early days of leading worship, back in the Church for the Nations). The whole quality of the worship shifts when you sing directly to Him, however simple the words. To worship is to abandon all personal pride and dignity, to be able to "be a fool" and not to care how you are perceived, as long as you are pleasing Him, just as David pleased the Lord even while scorned by his wife Michal, who thereafter suffered the curse of barrenness (see 2 Samuel 6:16–23).

Worship is the one thing in the spiritual realm that begins with us. Intercession starts in heaven, comes through our spirit, out of our mouths, and is thereby sown in the earth. Prophetic words and messages originate in heaven, come through God's prophets and ministers, and are declared to the people. But *worship* starts with *us*. Think about it. How could God be worshipped if worship started with God? He takes no pleasure in worshipping Himself but desires that all creation worship Him, the Creator of all things—visible and invisible.

It is not always wrong to begin in the *natural* realm to attain to the *spiritual* realm in worship. Most of us are familiar with the words of the nineteenth century British evangelist, Smith Wigglesworth, who said: "If the Spirit does not move me, I move the Spirit"; and we know what an "Apostle of Faith" Smith was! Worship comes out of a conscious decision to honor God. It is normally a choice we make or an appointment we keep. While the *choice* to worship, you might say, is made in the "natural" realm, God honors and nurtures that choice and comes to meet us more than half way, to draw us into the spiritual realm. And when the worshipper meets the Worshipped, the "natural" becomes spiritual.

Summing up

In whatever form or by whatever means, worship is focusing on God the Father and God the Son, through God the Holy Spirit, to the point of totally losing ourselves in Him—even to "being a fool" in the eyes of men.

B. WHY DO WE WORSHIP?

We need communication with God through Scriptures; we need communication with God through prayer; we need to enter into all that God is doing, according to our giftings and calling. But nothing will change us like worship. We're speaking here of *true* worship—deep, sincere, devoted, God-centered worship.

To lift Him up

Let us consider for a moment *why* we worship. When we begin to worship God, He comes on the scene to receive our worship. In turn we are blessed, because we're touched by His presence and our hearts are refilled with His inestimable love. But although we are transformed in and by His presence, we do not worship *in order* to feel good; we worship *not* to lift *ourselves* up but to lift *Him* up. It just follows that when we lift Him up, He lifts us up, as we rise up with wings like eagles (see Isaiah 40:31). So in turn, regardless of our focus on Him, we too are blessed!

To fill the bowls

We also worship to fill the "bowls" before the altar in heaven (see e.g., Zechariah 14:20; Revelation 8:5). Our worship and praise can be used by God—Father and Son—the object of our worship, as substance to be poured out as intercession on those that He knows to be most in need.

For example, Pastor Ruth Heflin of Mt. Zion Fellowship,[*] soon after founding her house of prayer in Jerusalem, had a visiting minister come and speak to their team. This guest preacher exhorted the young people to go out in the Holy City the next day and pass out tracts. Sister Ruth knew that in Jerusalem this is not acceptable practice, nor was it even lawful. She did not want to disappoint the twenty-five young people who had been challenged to "sow the seed" all across the city, so she sought wisdom from on high. That night she went to the Father and said, "Lord, give me Your answer for them." And in the middle of the night He answered her: "You sow heavenward, and I will sow earthward."

---

[*] The following testimony is from Ruth's first book, *Glory: A Jerusalem Experience* (Hagerstown, MD: McDougal, c.1990), 5–11.

Sister Ruth did not at first know what the Lord meant. But little by little, night by night, as they gathered for praise, He began to show them. As they moved into praise, the Lord would speak through a prophetic word: "Your praise delights Me. It thrills My heart. It pleases Me. But I want you to praise Me more." They gradually discovered that He wanted them not only to praise Him *more* but also to praise Him *louder*.

One night, after about six weeks of ever increasing and ever louder praise, enhanced by clapping and dancing and other ways of expressing praise and making a joyful noise, the Lord spoke to them: "Even now, while you are praising Me, I am pouring out My Spirit in another part of the city."

The next day they learned that the Holy Spirit had fallen on a social gathering of twenty-five young Arab Baptists, like on the Day of Pentecost, with the evidence of speaking in other tongues. Ruth said that, at that time in Jerusalem, twenty-five "was like two thousand, five hundred in the United States." This fruitful means of intercession led on to similar testimonies involving Gaza, Galilee, and other parts of Israel and beyond.

Look at what God can do with the substance of our worship. "The battle is the Lord's," but He wants us to furnish the ammunition. If we "sow to the heavens" (worship), He will "sow to the earth" (our worship returned as intercession). Since God turns the very essence of our worship into intercession to pour out upon and bless the earth wherever He sees the greatest need, we need to "sow" an abundance of worship. Empty bowls, no substance; no substance, angels sent forth with empty hands.

Even up through the last book of the Bible—the Book of Revelation—bowls are being filled with the intercession of the saints (see Revelation 8:5). This means it's up to us, having filled the bowls, to replenish them and keep them filled. If you want God to pour out on your city, the more substance you give Him, the more He has for sowing. We fill the bowls, and it is His messenger angels who deliver the goods. Isn't that good news? Isn't that simple? As Sister Ruth used to say: "there's an ease in the glory." Hallelujah!

Declarations

To suggest that the angels "deliver the goods" and that "the battle is the Lord's" is not to deny the fact that Spirit-led prayer, declarations, prophetic words, and even battle cries ought to come forth out of intercessory worship. The substance of our worship is only part of the story. We still have to be the Lord's hands and feet and voices in the earth. Even angels sometimes have to put things in our hands and give us a gentle push and a shove in the right direction.

It should follow naturally that, once you reach the heart of the Father in worship, He will put in your spirit—He will entrust to you—a word to declare into the earth, or into your city, or over the nations, or over timely issues that He has on His heart. If that word comes out of His Spirit, it will have power; if out of your spirit—or out of your head—no power. But if there are times when there is no spoken intercession, no matter; God is still using the substance of your worship to accomplish His purposes in the earth.

C. WHOM DO WE WORSHIP?

Whom do we worship? What a question! Of course we worship God. But do we worship God the Father, God the Son, and God the Holy Spirit? I personally believe that we do not worship the Holy Spirit. I believe that we worship the Father and the Son *by* the Spirit—by the power and leading of the Holy Spirit. The Holy Spirit is present in our worship and teaches us *how* to worship the Father and the Son, in ever new and creative ways.

As noted above, worship starts with *us*; but the Holy Spirit joins in together *with us* and guides us, as we seek to "worship the Father in spirit and in truth" (John 4:24). The Holy Spirit promises to teach us and to "guide [us] into all truth" (John 16:13). And in worship, we let the Holy Spirit take us wherever the Godhead wants us to go at any given moment.

We of course do not worship angels. This is not as self-evident as it may sound, so let us risk erring on the side of over-cautiousness here by recalling that John himself fell down and worshipped an angel:

> And I John saw these things, and heard them. And when I had heard and seen, I fell down to worship before the feet of the angel which shewed me these things. Then saith he unto me, See thou do it not: for I am thy fellowservant, and of thy brethren the prophets, and of them which keep the sayings of this book: worship God.
>
> —REVELATION 22:8–9

We are, of course, to worship neither angels nor saints, as is the misguided practice of some well-meaning souls. Only Jehovah God and Jesus/Yeshua Emmanuel are worthy to be worshipped—Father and Son. Angels do often delight to come and worship *with* us when they perceive an explosion of true adoration at even the smallest spot on the earth, and should be invited to do so. Since they come and go from before the throne of God, where they worship Him day and night, it is a special blessing and enrichment to have them singing and worshipping along with us in our gatherings. Welcome them in and acknowledge their presence. They are carriers of God's glory!

D. WHEN DO WE WORSHIP?

When do we worship? *All the time!* We should cultivate a *lifestyle of worship.* We can of course worship while driving; we can worship while walking down the street; we can worship in the bathroom, in the kitchen, in the laundry room; we can worship anywhere! We can and ought to maintain a lifestyle of worship.

However, if any of us should actually succeed in achieving such a lifestyle, that still does not substitute for quality time of dedicated worship, where we cut out all distractions and come aside to focus totally on Him. We need to *come away* with Him into the secret place (see Song of Solomon 2:10, 13). He wants *you.* He desires nothing more than He desires *you.*

Healing is wonderful; deliverance is wonderful; all the things from God are wonderful. But above all, *He* is wonderful. Relationship is what it's all about. He wants *our hearts* above *all things,* and as we pour out our hearts in worship, we discover *His heart.* So while worship ought to be a lifestyle, God the Father and God the Son desire that we also take time apart to meet with and worship Him (plural), by the Holy Spirit. Even Jesus Himself habitually drew aside to commune with His Father. How much more, then, ought we?

In a word, there really is no distinct "when." Father and Son are inestimably worthy, and both desire our unceasing worship. The angels round about the throne worship Him day and night—"24/7." As we are not yet in that place, it can help our self-discipline to have a regular time appointed to daily meet with Him for worship, in addition to reading His Word and listening. When you are faithful to this appointed time, you are likely to find Him already waiting for you there, in loving anticipation.

But waiting for you *where*? In your "special place," in the "secret place."

E. WHERE DO WE WORSHIP?

If the answer to "*When* do we worship?" is: "All the time," then surely the answer to "*Where* do we worship?" must be: "Everywhere"! No? Well, yes and no. Of course we can worship God anywhere at any time. We may worship Him spontaneously at those moments when we are suddenly aware of, and overcome by, the beauty of His creation—a sunset over the snowy peaks, a rainbow over a golden field, the morning glow over a misty lake; or when He has just snatched us from certain danger or delivered us from some impending evil or temptation. We will also worship at His feet whenever and wherever we encounter Him.

So is it really important to God *where* we worship? Do we really need a *regular* place of worship?

The "secret place" for individual worship

For the deeper more protracted times of worship, the intensely private times that may go on for hours, it is good to have a "place"—a "special place," a "secret place"—where you regularly meet with Him and He with you—a place where He is waiting for you and you are waiting on Him ("Wait, I say, on the Lord."—Psalm 27:14), and, to the extent possible, at a regular time.

I am reminded of the little fox in Saint Exupéry's *Le Petit Prince* (*The Little Prince*), where the fox asks the little prince to come to the same place every day at the same time, so that he (the fox) will have the double joy of, first, the anticipation and, then, the visit itself. "If you come at just any hour," says the fox, "I will never know when to prepare my heart."[*]

"But what if I don't have room for a 'secret place'?" There is *always* room for a "secret place."

Wherever I go, I try to find a place to live that, even if no more than an apartment, has one room with no walls that adjoin a neighbor. This is so that I can feel free in my expressions of praise and worship—even play my keyboard—without the thought of disturbing someone else or feeling constrained. Yet if this is not possible, a "secret place" need be no more than a corner of your living room, or a particular spot in your bedroom, or any other place of your choosing where you feel comfortable to meet one-on-One with the Master.

In my Washington DC apartment, for example, even though my study met my no-common-walls-with-any-neighbors criterion, I nonetheless found my "secret place" to be one particular spot in my living room where I somehow felt the most at peace in my spirit. This does not mean that I could not drop to my knees spontaneously, anywhere, at any time, or praise Him at any spot, in any room throughout my home. But that place in my living room became my "secret place," because that's where, alone at night, I was drawn to Him, where I sang to Him, where I spilled out my heart and my tears of love to Him, and where I listened for His still small voice. That spot was my "secret place."

In the Swiss farmhouse where I now live, I have a small

---

[*] Antoine de Saint-Exupéry, *Le Petit Prince* (Paris: Gallimard, 1946), 69–70.

dedicated prayer room—an ideally suited and furnished "upper room"—that serves no other purpose. Yet the place I most often find myself on my knees has turned out to be a certain spot downstairs in my living room. It is there that I most readily enter into His presence. That spot has thereby become my "secret place."

So there are no rules. You will discover your own "secret place," where you and the Holy Spirit like to meet and where you feel most comfortably at one with Him. There is no one who cannot have such a place. I believe you could have a "secret place" in the corner of a jail cell, if that's where you were to find yourself.

How does this all relate to corporate intercessory worship? Although your personal "secret place" is more suited to individual one-on-One worship, it is largely here that your spirit is nurtured and built up (edified) for breakthrough worship in concert with others. Your *corporate* intercessory worship will be fed by your *individual* "secret-place" worship. The power you bring to corporate breakthrough in the "special place" will depend largely on the intimate relationship you have developed in the "secret place."

The "special place" for corporate worship

So what about corporate worship? Does God care *where* we worship *together*? While again, anywhere we worship, He will come, He has certain locations where He wants to position us, for strategic reasons in the Spirit. It may be in the middle of the inner city, or it may be at the "gates"; it may be at the water's edge, or it may be on the "heights"; it may be in the heart of the financial district, or it may be in the midst of a slum; it may be in the shadow of the Parliament or Congress buildings, or it may be in the proximity of a prison; it may be in a church, or it may be in a soup kitchen. Father has a strategic place of prayer for every purpose under heaven.

Still, stay nimble; your strategic positioning is subject to change as the Spirit moves. But take care not to move out ahead of the cloud or the pillar of fire. He will show you when to move. *Follow the cloud, and when the cloud stands still, stay with the cloud!* (See Exodus 13:21; Numbers 14:14; Nehemiah 9:19.)

You will have read above how, progressively over the course of about a dozen years, Father moved our Breakthrough Worship ministry out of the Church for the Nations into a small chapel in the heart of Geneva's "inner city," then out to a 400-year-old chapel at the "gates" of Geneva, and ultimately up to a 700-year-old church on the "heights" of the Jura mountainside, overlooking the Lake of Geneva and on up the Lake to the very "City of God."

I believe that route was not coincidental. When we began in the Church for the Nations in central Geneva, we were not yet prepared for the assignments that were to follow. By the time Father eventually moved us up to the "heights," we were equipped for tougher missions.

For example, prior to our God-ordained move up to my little mountain village church, I had already sought the agreement of the pastor to let me transform an apparently unused small walled-off tower of the church into a dedicated prayer room. This walled-off area was formerly the apse which, along with churches throughout the cantons (provinces) that adopted Protestantism during the Protestant Reformation in Switzerland, had been cut off in the systematic eradication of every possible association with—and vestige of—Roman Catholicism. There is currently a move among the village churches in this canton to restore the apses that were thus lost.

With outside stairs leading up to what I visualized as an "upper room," I had long envisioned this as a "24/7" prayer tower. The pastor was favorable, even mildly enthusiastic, as he felt it coincided appropriately with the celebration of the 700th anniversary of this historic little church. But after making some enquiries with the (secular) village "Commune" administering this "annex," the pastor reported back that the space was already being used regularly by a music group / band, and the discussion stopped there.

Once God moved our Breakthrough Worship up to this village church, we came to discover that this "music group" was meeting in the little tower on the same night we were worshipping in the small sanctuary on the other side of the wall. Upon exiting the church at midnight, we could hear faint musical sounds, with muffled rhythmic beat, emanating from the tower.

One Breakthrough Worship night, after everyone had left, I approached the source of the sound and actually mounted the steps and slipped quietly through the unlocked door that I had never before found open. My objective for some time had been to propose a possible co-sharing of this room on different nights for our respective purposes. This seemed like my opportunity.

Once inside the outer door, I discovered inner doors, closing off a room where the "musicians" were assembled. I hesitated to go further because as I stood there I became aware, by the hollow repetitive sounds and heavy atmosphere, that apart from the eerie rhythmic recorded sounds, nothing seemed to be stirring in the room. I had never heard such sounds before and therefore recognized purely by the Spirit that this self-styled "band" was, in actual fact, a satanic worship group.

While disturbed that such activities were covertly going on virtually inside this church, under the guise of "band" practice, I did not feel free to expose the true nature of this group to the traditional Swiss pastor. I did share it with the breakthrough worshippers and announced that we would just carry on what Father brought us there to do. I had no fear, knowing that our God is greater. If we would but stay true to our assignment, the battle would be the Lord's, and by Him alone would be the victory.

When at some point we changed our meeting night (not on their account), it seems they soon thereafter changed their night to coincide—intentionally or not, we could not tell. We just carried on. We know our God.

Eventually, we no longer heard their dull rhythmic tones upon leaving the church at midnight. Whether in the end they changed their night to avoid us, or whether they left altogether, we may never know. But it is my belief that the power of God was too strong for them to perform their "rites" and that they had trouble operating while we were "breaking through" in worship on the other side of the wall. There is victory in the name of Jesus!

We have actually prayed consistently that this wall of partition come down and that the apse be restored to the church proper. One night, one of the worshippers suddenly pointed to tiny hairline cracks that had begun to appear in that wall—and that wall only, despite the fact that it is not even an outer wall exposed to wind and weather. It is indeed the only inner wall, and no water can plausibly seep in. These cracks have gradually grown more apparent and we are reminded of the walls of Jericho! We are happy to take full responsibility! Hallelujah!

I hasten to add that we are not at odds with the church in this regard. A special church Committee has now been set up to reclaim and restore the old apse to this history-steeped old church. The cracking wall has been duly noted by the Committee and serves as an added encouragement for them to persevere in prevailing upon the Commune to return the lost apse to the full custody of the church, to be restored to its original state.

Does God care *where* we worship? You, as a breakthrough worshipper, are strategic! You will know what He has called you to, because if He has chosen you to lead, He will reveal it to you personally, as you seek His guidance. And He will bring in those of like mind and heart, to whom He has given a similar burden and vision and holy boldness to break through.

Rest assured that He will not lead you into a place of danger until He has tested and strengthened you unto the task. He will lead you to the "special place" that corresponds to the assignment He has entrusted you with, and He will meet you there, with the angels to assist you. We should always bear in mind that there are three times as many angels as there are demons. Go confidently where He takes you and stay with the plan.

F. HOW DO WE WORSHIP?

One of my favorite Bible verses is the one mentioned earlier that says the Lord inhabits the praises of His people (see Psalm 22:3). I always assumed this to mean that, when we as His people praise together, God comes on the scene and tabernacles with us. Well, I still believe that, but have also experienced that when I open my mouth wide to cry out to Him in praise, His Spirit enters as if through that same open mouth and inhabits *me* (my spirit) through this sort of heaven-to-earth "shaft" opened up by my praises.

> Sing aloud unto God our strength: make a joyful noise unto the God of Jacob…open thy mouth wide, and I will fill it.
>
> —Psalm 81:1, 10

This infilling does not result from simply routinely singing a praise song! This results from truly opening up unreservedly and crying out / shouting out your praise. It needs to come out of the depths of your spirit—your innermost being—for His Spirit to inhabit your spirit in greater measure. It's as if His Spirit rushes in to fill the space created by the extravagant pouring forth of your praise! The more the praise flows out, the more His Spirit can flow in; and the more His Spirit flows in, the more the praise and effectual intercession can flow out! It's like a closed circuit with a Spirit-perpetuated never-ending stream.

Those who are unrestrained in their expressions of adoration to the Father and the Son, by the Holy Spirit, are likely to come up the highest and enter in the deepest and thereby discover most easily His heart for intercession. A powerful spiritual dynamic is released in corporate intercessory worship when *all* open up their mouths and together make a "loud noise"—a "joyful noise"—unto the Lord. He is faithful who promised that if we would do so, He would fill our mouths. Then we experience that He not only fills our mouth, but He fills our whole being in greater measure!

What a blessing it is to the Father's heart, and how refreshing it is to the worshipper, as we come and open up freely to Him and praise Him with our whole being, unreservedly, in childlike abandon. Father loves our praise, and if you don't praise Him, the stones will cry out! He *will* be praised!

Entering into His gates

The Word says we are to *"[e]nter into His gates with thanksgiving, and into His courts with praise"* (Ps. 100:4). The *gates* are wonderful, and we should approach them with thanksgiving! The *outer courts* are wonderful, and we are to enter them with high praise! *Praise* is wonderful, and it breaks open the heavens as well as our own hearts, and focuses our thoughts on Him who is worthy. But it is ultimately through the *inner court*, into the *holy place*, and on into the *holy of holies*, where we fall down at His feet and truly worship. As worshippers, that's where we passionately desire to come—into the holy place, into the holy of holies. That's where we find the greatest intimacy and rest, after the intercessory victory has been won in the inner court.

Although we often speak and sing of the "sacrifice of praise" (see Jeremiah 33:11), it is a glorious "sacrifice" when the praises arise out of the joy of the Lord. The "sacrifice" of praise is not grievous.

Ruth Heflin, in her book *Glory,*[*] writes about how her spirit was disturbed by the phrase "praise the Lord anyhow", which implies that you should praise God whether you feel like it or not. (I would add: perhaps even *especially* if you are feeling down and out and yet, while unable to rise to the level of heartfelt praise, want to acknowledge that you know you *should* be "praising anyway.")

---

[*] Heflin, *Glory,* 11ff.

I cannot help but be reminded of the "Happy Bird Song" from my childhood:

> Just sing a happy little song
> When any little thing goes wrong.
> Be as happy as can be
> Just fill yourself with glee
> When any little thing goes wrong.

Yet when something suddenly went wrong for the Happy Bird, he had to be admonished by his friends to just sing his happy little song "anyhow." He complied, but his voice clearly revealed that his heart was far from it.

Sister Ruth, upon seeking the Lord over her discomfort with this popular phrase, "praise the Lord anyhow," was led by the Holy Spirit to the Old Testament where any sacrifice offered to God had to be perfect, without blemish. Yet "we were being taught," she writes, "that we could offer any old praise to God and that it would be accepted."[**]

How much more, given the added intimacy inherent in worship, ought we to approach the inner court in all holiness.

Praise as distinguished from worship

It should be pointed out here that, while praise and worship belong together, they are *not* one and the same thing. Praise can and should lead into worship—indeed, be an integral part of worship. But while praise is a form of worship and worship a form of praise, they are not to be seen as equivalent expressions of homage to God.

Consider the Levites:

[**]   Ibid.

> ...Hezekiah the king and the princes commanded
> the Levites to sing praise unto the LORD with the
> words of David, and of Asaph the seer. And they
> *sang praises* with gladness, *and* they *bowed their
> heads and worshipped.*
>
> —2 Chronicles 29:30, emphasis added

Intercession should be an *outcome* of high praise and active worship, at the same time as the praise and worship provide the very *essence* of the intercession itself. It is in that atmosphere of heaven brought down that we can best hear the Father's heart to enable us to declare it, to enable us to effectively "prophesy unto the wind" (Ezek. 37:9), to inspire effectual Spirit-led intercession. Because if we do not get the Father's heart, we can intercede all night, and it goes no higher than the ceiling.

Basically, praise is for the outer court and worship is for the inner court, and ultimately on into the holy place and the holy of holies, where we desire ultimately to abide.

Entering into the inner court

So how do we move from the outer court of praise to the inner court where we can reach the Father's heart to effectively intercede His purposes? Through worship—heartfelt, spontaneous worship—flowing out of high praises; by singing spontaneous "new songs" as well as familiar songs sung out of the hearts and spirits of anointed psalmists, singers, musicians; by dancing, with both joy and reverence, before Him; by bowing down before Him; by lifting holy hands up to Him; by crying out to Him, our Beloved; by honoring Him with all that we are and have in us, including our substance (offerings). Indeed, how can we encounter His most holy presence as He receives our praise and *not* experience the spontaneous response of adulation?

> Give unto the Lord the glory due unto his name: bring an offering, and come before him: worship the Lord in the beauty of holiness.
>
> —1 Chronicles 16:29

So we start at the gates with thanksgiving and move into the outer court with praise. Then the Holy Spirit leads us, little by little, through to the inner court.

We're talking of the temple now. The temple was considered the ultimate place of worship and was itself a symbol of worship. It was surrounded by outer courts with one gate only. Within the inner court was the temple with two chambers separated by a veil. The first chamber, outside the veil, was the holy place; the second chamber, inside the veil, was the holy of holies, containing the ark of the covenant and the mercy seat. Only the high priest could enter the holy of holies, and only once a year, on the Day of Atonement.

Access to the holy of holies

But the very moment of Jesus's death on the cross, making the ultimate sacrificial once-for-all atonement for the whole of mankind, the seamless veil of the temple was torn in two from top to bottom (see Matthew 27:50–51), signifying that we ourselves now, as a holy priesthood, have access to the very holy of holies.

> Having therefore, brethren, boldness to enter into the holiest by the blood of Jesus, By a new and living

way, which he hath consecrated for us, through the
veil, that is to say, his flesh.

—Hebrews 10:19–20

The rending of the veil, offering access to the "brethren,"
does not mean that the holy of holies became any less sacrosanct than when the Lord said to Moses:

Speak unto Aaron thy brother, that he come not at
all times [i.e., at just any time] into the holy place
within the vail before the mercy seat, which is upon
the ark; that he die not [i.e., lest he die!].

—Leviticus 16:2

We must take care not to enter in casually or without
thoughtful preparation. Defiling the holy place is a very
serious matter—even unto death (in the Old Testament,
at least).

Cleansing ourselves

Just as Esther cleansed herself for one year to go in unto
the king, and later—even as queen—fasted for three days
to go before her royal husband, she still had to wait until
he held out his scepter to her before she was allowed to
approach (see Esther 2:12, 4:15–5:2). How much more need
we to cleanse ourselves before approaching the King of
kings, before entering the holiest of holies? We want to
hear Him say, "approach, My beloved," because it is in the
holy of holies that we will experience the greatest intimacy.
It is here that we will find our closest communion with
the King.

How thankful we are that Jesus does not require of
us the months of preparation required of Esther before
entering the king's chambers. Yet He does require of us

cleansing. In the temple, between the outer court and the inner court, there is a laver—a bowl of water. So any who make it through the gate and the outer court without cleansing themselves still have to wash before going on into the inner court and into the holy place.

Not everyone comes into the holy of holies. You must come with clean hands, because it is very, very holy. You must come with a clean heart, because it is very, very holy. You must come with clean lips, because it is very, very holy. You must come in humility, because those who are not pure in heart shall not see God (see Matthew 5:8). Cleansing is essential, and it comes through true repentance.

Joshua himself, the high priest, with access to the very holy of holies, once stood before the angel of the Lord in filthy garments (see Zechariah 3:3). While in his filthy garments, Satan was free to stand next to him (v. 1)! The angel associated the filthy garments with iniquity and ordered that they be removed, thereby symbolically releasing Joshua from his sin (v. 4). This high priest was then clothed with new garments and only then did the angel of the Lord stand with him (v. 5), declaring to him that if he would walk in the Lord's ways, he would judge the house and courts of the Lord! First repentance; afterward the house and courts of the Lord.

So before we even approach the outer gates, we should have already been preparing ourselves. We will not want to halt between the outer and inner court—or between the inner court and the holy of holies—to repent before the Lord. This should be done even prior to entering the gates!

The place of repentance

Repenting is not something we do only one time, as when we are first "saved." Repentance is for every day.

We may have to repent *several* times a day, and especially before entering into warfare. It is not for our former or greatest sins that we need to repent repeatedly; it is repentance for critical or impure thoughts; for a particular action or inaction, or omission; for any hint of pride; for a harsh word; for an impatient, unkind, selfish, or thoughtless act or gesture.

We have to come to the gates with clean lips and clean hands, with a clean heart and a clear conscience. Otherwise we do not enter the inner court, spiritually. We can stay in the outer court and praise; we can do that; but we cannot go on through the inner court and ultimately on in to the holy of holies, the secret place. Even for the outer court of praise, we should be mindful of where we are and before whom we are coming.

King Saul himself understood that he could not worship the Lord unless he first repented of his disobedience. Speaking to Samuel, King Saul said:

> Now therefore, I pray thee, *pardon my sin*, and turn again with me, *that I may worship the Lord.*
> —1 SAMUEL 15:25, EMPHASIS ADDED

And heed the Word of the Lord to Jeremiah:

> Stand in the gate of the LORD's house, and proclaim there this word, and say, Hear the word of the LORD, all ye of Judah, that enter in at these gates to worship the LORD. Thus saith the LORD of hosts, the God of Israel, *Amend your ways and your doings, and I will cause you to dwell in this place.*
>
> Trust ye not in lying words, saying, The temple of the LORD, The temple of the LORD, The temple of the LORD, are these. For if ye throughly *amend*

your ways and your doings; if ye throughly execute judgment between a man and his neighbour; If ye oppress not the stranger, the fatherless, and the widow, and shed not innocent blood in this place, neither walk after other gods to your hurt: *Then* will I *cause you to dwell in this place*, in the land that I gave to your fathers, for ever and ever.
—JEREMIAH 7:2–7, EMPHASIS ADDED

All who were to enter the gates of the temple were exhorted by God Himself, through His prophet Jeremiah, to amend their evil ways—not only the obvious sin of murder, the shedding of innocent blood, but even patently lesser wrongs such as oppressing the stranger or the widow. We all know that to *repent* means not only to ask forgiveness but to be truly remorseful before a holy God and to cease from the unrighteous act, thought, or omission.

When the children of Israel returned from captivity:

they stood up in their place, and read in the book of the law of the LORD their God one fourth part of the day; and another *fourth part [of the day]* they *confessed*, and *worshipped* the LORD their God.
—NEHEMIAH 9:3, EMPHASIS ADDED

First they confessed, and *then* they worshipped.

"Yes," you say, "but we are living under the New Covenant, and in the twenty-first century; surely we are under grace!" Times may change; we may change; even grace may "much more abound," through the cross and blood of Jesus Christ. But has God Almighty changed? Is He any less holy? His Word says that He is "the same yesterday, and to day [sic], and for ever" (Heb. 13:8). He also says, "For I am the LORD, I change not" (Mal. 3:6). Should we honor and respect Him any less because of His abundant grace?

I like what David Adeola writes in his book *City Gates* in the Year of our Lord 2013:

> The Bible clearly states that we cannot come to the house of the Lord and enter the gate of the Temple to come and worship the Lord with our filth and sin. God makes clear that we need to amend our ways before we approach the gates to come and worship.
>
> As a believer and child of God you cannot approach the gates of worship any[old]how! As you cannot come before an earthly monarch without observing the necessary protocol, you'll be marched out by security for breaking protocol. How much more the King of Kings who is supreme over all things?*

We all know that God is love, and we may think that He cannot refuse any free-will offering, but remember that He did not accept the offering of Cain because he did not offer his *firstfruits*—his *best* offering (see Genesis 4:3–7). Certainly, "the LORD looketh on the heart" (1 Sam. 16:7) and He accepts us as we are, in whatever circumstance we find ourselves, especially when we are babes. But as we grow, He expects more from us, as any good and caring father would; and He is indeed worthy to be honored with our *best*. "Who honors God, God honors."** Do we honor Him by being casual in our response to His monumental sacrifice of the very blood of His dear Son, Jesus Christ? Is

---

* David Adeola, *City Gates: Watching Over the City Gates* (Singapore: n.p., 2013), 90–91.
** A quote from *Chariots of Fire*, a 1981 British film, based on a true story from the 1924 Olympics. [*Chariots of Fire*, directed by Hugh Hudson (1981; Los Angeles, CA: 20th Century Fox, 2005), DVD.]

it too much to expect of us to pay Him the reverence that is due His Majesty?

God is every bit as holy and supreme now as He was in Old Testament times—the same yesterday, today, and forever. We are well aware that before Jesus's resurrection caused the veil of the temple to be torn in two, opening the way for all believers to enter the holy of holies, only the high priest could enter in, and only once a year. The fact that believers now have unrestricted access to the holiest of holies does not make it any less sacrosanct. It does not mean that we, accorded this amazing grace and unlimited access, can therefore enter in casually or just any way we please.

If the Lord was attentive to the state of the (spiritual) *garments* of even Joshua, the high priest himself, who are we to set or accept a different standard for ourselves as priestly intercessors? We should be "all the children of light" (1 Thess. 5:5).

> But ye are a chosen generation, a royal priesthood, an holy nation, a peculiar people; that ye should shew forth the praises of him who hath called you out of darkness into his marvellous light.
>
> —1 Peter 2:9

Indeed, as a holy priesthood, we are not only to carry God's heart, but we are also to radiate His presence. God can neither fully entrust us with His heart of intercession nor manifest His full glory through us if we harbor impurities in our minds or hearts. He does not require that we spend hours agonizing over our sins. He is quick to forgive a sincere and truly penitent heart. But repentance is an essential prerequisite to entering the holy of holies.

Entering in corporately

If you are in a corporate setting, do not allow yourself to be put off by pride or embarrassment that others might overhear your repentance. Everyone should be exhorted to become absorbed in their own repentance and ignore everything and everyone around them. You don't need to be loud with God, as you may need to be at times with the enemy. While the enemy is hard of hearing, God has a still small voice—and impeccable reception.

Now, when you have repented, washed your hands, and come into the inner court, there are things you must not do. If you do them, you come back out, and, when in a corporate setting, you may bring everyone else back out with you. Because when the sanctity is defiled, the atmosphere is defiled, and everyone is affected.

This is simply meant to re-emphasize that the inner court is already a place of holiness before the Lord. And it is to say that if you want to maintain the atmosphere—if you want to stay in the inner court and move on to the holy place—then there are certain things you must observe, especially in the company of other worshippers: first and foremost, no talking; I mean, *no* talking, not even a whisper.[*]

When the worship is at its most intimate, you may find you cannot even move without disturbing the Spirit. There must be an awesome respect for His holy presence; and this is something you learn, by the Spirit; you don't fall straight into the holy of holies. But if you know this much, then you are on your way into the secret place. Because if you *do not* know this, then when other worshippers enter the holy place, you can break the anointing for everyone, especially in a small group. You can pull everyone back

---

[*] See below, subsection under "D. WHEN do we worship?"

out. And if you are brought out through a lack of respect toward the Holy Spirit, it can be a long way back in, if at all, both for you and for the others as well.

Accordingly, when leading worship—whether all night or for three hours—my own objective, my ultimate goal, is for everyone to "enter in" and then *stay* there at the throne until we have the heart of the Father—not run in and out, in and out, as often unwittingly is the case. It is a very long night if we are going in and out of the inner court and have to keep going back to the gates. It is a very long night if someone walks out of the room to make coffee when others are between the outer and the inner court, or moving on into the holy of holies. Because by the time we come into the holy place, it is very, very holy; and it is the holy of holies where we find the greatest intimacy with Him. *That is where we are truly changed.*

By the time we enter the holy of holies, we are no longer crying out or declaring prophetically into the earth. We are usually prostrate and silent before His overwhelming presence. The praise has already largely died out in the outer court; intercession has already been largely accomplished in the inner court; and the deepest worship often comes after the combat, following the victory and the accompanying sense of joy and exultation. But God is not constrained by any single format or formula. The important thing is to be "in the Spirit," in order to intercede effectively—whether out of worship or out of high praise.

Bold versus gentle intercessory worship

When intercessory worship comes forth out of the high praises, it may take the form of war dances in the Spirit or marches leading us into heavy spiritual combat, in and by the Holy Spirit. And since "the battle is the Lord's," we can experience jubilation and even exuberance in the midst of the battle!

> And when he had consulted with the people, he appointed *singers* unto the LORD, and that should praise the beauty of holiness, as they *went out before the army*, and to say, Praise the LORD; for his mercy endureth for ever. And *when they began to sing and to praise, the Lord set ambushments* against the children of Ammon, Moab, and mount Seir, which were come against Judah; *and they were smitten.*
> —2 CHRONICLES 20:21–22, EMPHASIS ADDED

And we are all familiar with the way in which the praisers were sent before the army to bring down the walls of Jericho. (See Joshua 5:13–6:27.)

It is important also to keep in mind that there can be *warfare worship* as powerful as *spiritual warfare out of high praise!* We are told that "when we *worship*, the *Lion of Judah roars!*" When we truly worship, by the Spirit, the Lord will fight for us (see Deuteronomy 20:4), for "the battle is the LORD's" (1 Sam. 17:47)!

But even quieter worship may move, in a new wave, back into a crescendo of high praise, out of which may proceed renewed intercession, even wave after wave. What is important is following wherever the Holy Spirit goes. He will orchestrate your intercession—individually and corporately—to accomplish His purposes under heaven.

In our experience in Geneva, we became freer and freer in our praise and worship. Freer may mean louder; freer may mean bolder; bolder may mean more powerful. But this in no way denigrates the potential power of softer worship, which should not be seen as less effectual for intercession than high praise, simply because it may be at a lower decibel. We have sometimes sensed His greatest pleasure in our quietest times of worship.

Ruth Heflin, mentioned earlier, who had a house of prayer in Jerusalem (she is now in an eternal house of prayer in heaven), used to say, "Praise until the worship comes, worship until the glory comes, and then stand in the glory." We somewhat adopted that as a "watchword" for our intercessory worship in Geneva. But over time this effectively evolved into something more like: praise until the worship comes, worship until the intercession comes, and "prophesy unto the wind" (Ezek. 37:9); then fall down and worship in the glory.

Be it out of praise or out of worship, as the Spirit leads, we should be making declarations over our city and the nations, or whatever the Father reveals to us of what is on His heart! This can at times be very bold, loud, and warfare-like; but worship warfare can even be waged without words. Whether out of worship or high praise, it matters little, as long as it is by, with, and of the Holy Ghost.

Singing unto the Lord

> O come, let us sing unto the Lord: let us make a joyful noise to the rock of our salvation. Let us come before his presence with thanksgiving, and make a joyful noise unto him with psalms. For the Lord is a great God, and a great King above all gods.
>
> —Psalm 95:1–3

One of the purest and simplest ways to worship God is to sing to Him. He loves to hear your song. When you sing to the Lord, it doesn't matter at all what your voice sounds like. It doesn't matter if you have a beautiful voice or if you are even in tune. Not at all. God just wants to hear your voice! He takes pleasure in hearing your joyful *sound!* So simply "[m]ake *a joyful noise* unto the Lord" (Ps. 100:1, emphasis added).

Are you a mother or a father? Let's say your little child starts to sing—totally out of tune. How do you feel? Don't you just *love* his song? Isn't it *beautiful* to you? Then how about our heavenly Father—holy Father God—the perfect Father? He *loves* your voice. He doesn't care if you are off tune or hit wrong notes. He just desires to hear your voice, directed toward His attentive ear.

As you worship, listen for notes from heaven and then sing them out. Sounds from heaven carry power, carry breakthrough. He gives you the sound to release into the earth to accomplish His purposes. *Open your mouth wide and He will fill it!* This familiar verse from the psalms is indeed pronounced in the very context of worship:

> There shall no strange god be in thee; neither shalt thou *worship* any strange god. I am the Lord thy God, which brought thee out of the land of Egypt: *open thy mouth wide, and I will fill it.*
> —Psalm 81:9–10, emphasis added

When the Lord your God fills your mouth, speak! Sing! Shout! Declare! Intercede! Don't be held back by pride or fear of hitting a wrong note. You will be surprised at new harmonies that you never would have imagined! While worshipping in song, I may hear in my spirit a note that I am sure will be discordant, but, in daring to sing it out, discover it to be amazingly harmonious, with a wholly new harmony, a distinctive fresh harmony I have never heard before. If I am timid, it doesn't work. Be bold! He creates new sounds from heaven that are beyond our remotest conception.

Scott Hicks of True Worship Ministries writes:[*]

> Scripture says: "Out of the mouths of babes and suckling have I perfected praise" Matthew 21:16. I heard someone say about this Scripture, "Praise is not perfected when it leaves our mouth; it's perfected when it enters His ears—because He has perfected it."

Reading this suddenly took me back to my Washington DC apartment where, alone in my living room at night, I would worship and sing to the Lord. I had always been blessed with good pitch and a facility to carry a tune—even to harmonize naturally—but never possessed what anyone would characterize as a beautiful voice. In fact, I can recall my closest cousin, an economist who sang tenor professionally as a hobby, telling me expressly—while out rowing on the lake one night at our family summer place, where I must have ventured to sing along out of pure conviviality—that I would "never be a singer." Actually, I had never presumed to be or to become one, and it seemed a bit gratuitous to thus bluntly remind me. But years later, that same cousin—not given to facile compliments, especially where it came to singing—told me that I had "a very pretty voice."

What had happened? Well, as I sang to the Lord in my simple way in my living room in DC, fully conscious of my vocal shortcomings, I began to ask the Lord to make my voice beautiful *for Him*. I prayed to this effect: "Father, it doesn't really matter what my voice sounds like all alone

---

[*] Scott Hicks, "A New Sound is Coming to the Church! Christian Music will Receive a Praise and Worship 'Face Lift,'" March 1, 2008.

in this living room, but please just change it on its way up to You so that when it reaches Your ear, it is beautiful." This satisfied me, and I continued to pray in this manner each time I sang to Him.

Then one night while I was singing, I heard—for just a moment—an unfamiliar voice, a surprisingly pretty voice; and lo and behold it was coming out of *my* mouth. It lasted for only a few notes, but it quite surprised me and afforded me a momentary thrill. As I carried on in my nightly singing to the Lord, I noticed this "new" voice beginning to continue on a little longer, then yet a little longer. I could actually objectively enjoy the sound of my own voice singing unto the Lord.

My voice took on this new quality only in my private worship times—only when I was singing alone to my Beloved in the "secret place." Gradually, however, it extended to worship beyond the "secret place," but still only in the presence of the Lord and under His anointing. For example, in a church setting, total strangers would turn around and tell me I had a lovely voice, or even approach me after a service to tell me so personally.

Over time, this new voice became more or less my "real" voice, but it is still not perfected. It's the anointing on the voice, not the voice itself, that leads the worship higher. My voice is still at its best in the anointing, when freely and joyously leading praise and worship with abandon, in the fullness of the Spirit. The singing comes forth by the anointing, and the anointing comes forth by the singing.

> Hear, O ye kings; give ear, O ye princes; I, even I, will sing unto the LORD; I will sing praise to the LORD God of Israel.
>
> —JUDGES 5:3

So nothing is impossible with God, especially when our highest desire is to please and to minister unto Him. To effectively lead worship into realms of glory, the anointing must be on the voice. Sing to Him and you will see for yourself.

Dancing before the Lord

There are many expressions of the dance in worship: spontaneous dance, by an individual or by any number of worshippers; choreographed dance, by an individual or a company of dancers; group dancing, such as extemporaneous circle- or line-dancing, or other forms of movement that involve everyone and help to create unity and generate an atmosphere of joyfulness and praise.

Sister Ruth Heflin, at her House of Prayer in Jerusalem, regularly included the dance from the very outset of each gathering—everyone joining in together, usually in the form of a circle in motion—letting the Holy Spirit take over from there. In fact that essentially *was* the prayer meeting. There was always movement. She believed that dancing brings an anointing for the nations. Well, I don't know about you, but I want the nations for an inheritance! (See Psalm 2:8.) So I dance, led by the Holy Spirit, because it serves as effectual intercession, but also simply because it is part of the spontaneous joy of high praises unto God Almighty.

I also dance because David danced and it pleased the Lord. David did not dance *in order* to please the Lord; he danced with all his might *because of* his sheer gladness at bringing up the ark of God to Jerusalem and because the Spirit of God was upon Him. And the fact that he yielded to that Spirit without regard for the opinion of man was pleasing to God.

No, David was not dancing in order to please God or man, nor was he dancing in order to attract attention or admiration. In fact, in his wife Michal's eyes, he was making an utter fool of himself. Yet he pleased God by his "foolish" abandon. We need to drop our self-consciousness and become God-conscious in our worship. Which would you rather experience—Michal's punishment or David's reward?

When I myself first began to move into this whole process of getting freer and more expressive in praise and worship, I started with no more than a somewhat tentative lifting of my hands, about waist-high, palms up, sheltered from view by the person in front of me so as not to be noticed. This reflected quite accurately where I was spiritually at that point. Much further along in my spiritual evolution, my hands would spontaneously raise *themselves* up high, as it were, with no prompting at all, in open and abandoned expression of my heartfelt praises to God my Maker.

Similarly, as regards dancing before the Lord, I could not make myself dance simply because others were doing so or because it was expected of me. In my case, the "dance" first occurred spontaneously at a conference in Washington DC, in the midst of praise and worship, while singing "Blow the Trumpet in Zion"! I just suddenly found myself dancing in place at my seat—nothing remarkable, just little hop-steps of joy. It was the joy of the Lord, translated without aforethought into corresponding physical expression.

It doesn't matter if your dance step never gets beyond simply moving your feet. That qualifies! Ruth Heflin used to say, "If you have that dance in your feet, you will have an anointing to feed the bread, the meat, the wine, unto the nations."* She professes to have danced in the toilets of 707s, 747s and DC10s. How? "Straight up and down" she explains.** That suffices to tread on serpents and scorpions and over all the power of the enemy (see Luke 10:19)!

Your "dance" does not have to be graceful or refined, and it does not matter who is or is not watching. I dance whenever the Spirit moves me, like David, willing to appear a fool. I have sometimes found myself leaping—springing higher, with greater ease, than I could ever do naturally, and I no longer care who might see. It is both from and unto the Lord.

I can recall a definite point in time where I took a decisive step forward in ceasing to care what people see or think of me when I am in worship, if otherwise I might offend the Holy Spirit or be drawn away prematurely. At the end of praise and worship, lost in the presence of God, eyes still closed, I became aware that others were beginning to be seated, all around; but my spirit was not ready to sit down. I did not want to stand out by not following suit, but at that instant I determined, once and for all, that it was more important where I was with Father God at that moment than what other people might think. That was for me a milestone in freedom, and I never went back to being fearful about embarrassing myself or possibly offending others, if it could mean risking offending my Father or His Holy Spirit. I have since become persuaded that, in fact, no-one even takes any notice.

Freedom from what others may think of us applies to all aspects of our praise and worship—whether it be our posture, whether it be our voice, whether it be our dance or other movements flowing out naturally from within, or

---

* Heflin, *Glory*, 25.
** Ibid.

any other form our praise and worship might take, by the Spirit. We need to forget about ourselves and those around us and simply lose ourselves in Him. Be free!

G. WITH WHOM DO WE WORSHIP?

On the personal level, as noted earlier, we want to embrace a lifestyle of worship. We want to maintain an attitude of worship as well as to set aside regular times of dedicated worship where we privately engage in strictly bilateral communion with the Lord. If Jesus Himself habitually drew apart to commune with Father God, how can we presume to do any less?

The power of unity

Yet we also need to come together as a group. There is extra power when the people of God get together to pray. There is added strength in numbers where there is unity, and this can release a special corporate anointing.

It is written that "where two or three are gathered together in [His] name, there [He is] in the midst of them" (Matt. 18:20). We are told that even one can chase a thousand and two alone can put ten thousand to flight (see Deuteronomy 32:30). Further, five can chase a hundred, and a hundred can put ten thousand to flight (Lev. 26:8)! So a room full of intercessory worshippers should be able to put tens of thousands to flight—across your city, your nation, and the nations of the earth! It has been said that "prayer moves mountains; combined prayer moves nations!"[*]

Even in a corporate setting, the personal aspect of

____

[*]   Suzette Hattingh, "The Porch and the Altar" (presented at the Mission Possible Conference, Zelhem, The Netherlands, October 22–27, 2013).

worship is not sacrificed. Each one should be led individually by the Spirit of God, and as each one is in tune with the Spirit, the spirit of unity will come and make all one. Individuality melds into unity, which is paramount in corporate intercession.

I see the oneness as resulting not from a person-to-person ("horizontal") connection but from a room full of person-to-God ("vertical") connections reaching up together as one. So while worship is essentially a very personal thing between you and God, when His people come together, if they are in unity, they have the potential for unfathomable intercessory power.

Consider the Tower of Babel where, even when *rebellious* people were unified by one language, God said that nothing would be impossible to them (Gen. 11:6). Just imagine, then, with a room full of intercessors, unified by the Holy Spirit, the unlimited possibilities available to the *people of God!*

In our original Geneva group of all-night intercession, I used to share a brief teaching before entering into corporate praise and worship—not only for us to learn and grow together but to bring us into a unity of mind and spirit for that night.

Over time, when we began to meet weekly for three hours instead of monthly for all night, I gradually dispensed with the teaching in favor of entering directly into praise and worship—impatient to use the full time for joining with the Holy Spirit in making our way to the throne through intercessory worship. This was sometimes preceded by an opening prayer, and sometimes the prayer just naturally emerged out of the opening worship.

Either way, truly "entering in" often necessitated considerable time to cleanse and sanctify both the premises and ourselves—through the prayer, repentance, and praise and worship itself—before we could actually rise to the level of the throne. Now, years later, with numbers reduced over time to the most faithful, we sense that the angels are already waiting, and it takes little or no time at all to climb to the heavenly realms.

Individual and/or corporate repentance is still a part of this process. But if we come together already in a substantially cleansed, sanctified, forgiving, and forgiven state, this greatly accelerates our approach and entrance through the gates of thanksgiving into the courts of praise, and ultimately on into the holy of holies.

Corporately, there is a "spirit of worship"—the atmosphere that is created by the Spirit of God when we worship in one accord—that further promotes our flowing in unity. We continue to invite the Holy Spirit to show us new ways to worship and to teach us how better to worship God "in spirit and in truth."

Climbing the holy hill together

We have found that one of the most effective ways to enter into corporate worship and come into unity is to start by joining together in "singing in the Spirit," where our many voices are supernaturally brought into perfect harmony because it is not some *twenty-five* spirits; it is *one* Spirit. When we *all* sing in the Spirit, the many meld into *one*, and then we are ready to do exploits—together! To climb the holy hill together, to take territory together, to shake cities together. Corporate intercession!

One all-night prayer meeting in Geneva will always live in my memory. On that particular night—it was toward the beginning of our regular all-night prayer gatherings—we (men and women) began as usual to sing in the Spirit in order to come into unity in preparation for praying for the nations. For some reason it was particularly difficult that night; it was very "heavy going." Sometimes the heavens are open, and other times the heavens seem like brass (though the brass is often not the heavens but rather ourselves, arriving with all our "baggage" and unresolved issues).

This night the heavens seemed like brass. But we sang and we sang in the Spirit, pushing forward. No harmony, discordant voices (there are of course no discordant voices to God, but the human ear is less forgiving...) and no perceivable "flow."

It seemed a real struggle, but we kept on. We just carried on singing in the Spirit, and we slowly but slowly started to ascend, little by little, step by step. It was as if we were climbing up a rugged mountain. It was very steep, with lots of rocks, lots of tree roots, lots of obstacles. We were trying to make our way uphill, clamoring ever upward. We were stumbling over rocks; we were catching our feet in tree roots and picking our way with uncertain step, over uneven ground. But we kept going; we kept on—up, up, up—over rutted and difficult terrain. But the important thing is, we didn't stop; we all kept pushing onward, upward, all the while singing in the Spirit.

Then all of a sudden, it was as if we broke out at the top. And there was that heavenly harmony that was a treat to the ear and an excitement to the spirit. We had *made it* to the *top!* And you know what was up there? The throne of God...the very throne of God! We had made it, and the harmony broke out freely and unreservedly.

> And it came to pass, that when David was come to
> the top of the mount…he worshipped God…
> —2 Samuel 15:32

That's where we always want to go in our worship. That's where we're *always* aiming to go—to the throne of God, to get His heart—whether through the outer and inner courts or up the mountain of God. We want to worship with the angels at the throne, where they worship day and night.

So whenever we at last arrive at the throne of God, it has sometimes been a long journey; sometimes it's a very hard climb to the throne. But when we get there, *glory!* There's an ease in the glory! I want to stay there. I want to dwell awhile in the holy place:

> He that dwelleth in the secret place of the most
> High shall abide under the shadow of the Almighty.
> —Psalm 91:1

So when it comes to worship, whether we speak of the "inner court," the "holy place," the "holy of holies," or the "mountaintop," spiritually we are speaking about coming to His throne, into His very presence, to His very footstool, even into His very chambers. Wherever the throne is found (through true worship), that is a holy place. Take off your shoes, for the ground on which you stand is holy (see Exodus 3:5). Having made it, rest awhile and commune with the King. Abide under the shadow of the Almighty, tune your ear to Him, and listen for His heart of intercession.

Whenever and wherever we come to His feet and fall down to worship Him, that, spiritually, is His throne. This does not negate the fact that He has an actual throne in heaven[*] or that He will have a real throne on earth in the New Jerusalem.^{**} But until we are actually in either of those places "physically," our worship brings us, spiritually, to His throne—whether hilltop or holy place.

> Who shall ascend into the hill of the LORD? or who
> shall stand in his holy place?
>
> —PSALM 24:3

As regards resting awhile in the holy place once you get there, I like to use the following illustration: Suppose I have an invitation from the president of the United States, and I make a long and perhaps arduous journey to get to the White House. I am finally ushered in through the gate, showing my pass, on through security, and at last arrive at the renowned Oval Office, where the president is seated. Yet once I get there, after all the effort and obstacles, I just stand outside the door and don't go in to meet with the president. That doesn't make a lot of sense. Or if I stand there and just make a little "hi sign" and then quickly retreat, the entire undertaking, effort, and anticipation will largely have been in vain. Even if the journey has in fact been a pleasant one, my highly valued and anticipated encounter will remain unrealized. It is not the journey there but rather the time I spend with the president, once

---

* The throne in heaven: "The LORD is in his holy temple, *the Lord's throne is in heaven*" (Ps. 11:4). "The LORD hath prepared his *throne in the heavens*; and his kingdom ruleth over all" (Ps. 103:19). "And immediately I was in the spirit: and, behold, *a throne was set in heaven*, and one sat on the throne" (Rev. 4:2). (Emphases added).

** The throne on earth in the New Jerusalem: "And he shewed me a pure river of water of life, clear as crystal, *proceeding out of the throne of God and of the Lamb*" (Rev. 22:1). "And there shall be no more curse: *but the throne of God and of the Lamb shall be in it*; and his servants shall serve him" (Rev. 22:3). (Emphases added).

I have arrived, that matters most. So when we persevere and actually get there, let's enter in, and let's stay awhile.

Now, to move on, we need to remind ourselves that even if corporate worship fosters solidarity, it is not about us. There is nothing "horizontal" about it; it is all "vertical"; it is all about Him. But as stated earlier, instead of just one "vertical," it is a room full of "verticals" joining together as one. The more connections to the Source, the greater the flow of the Spirit; the greater the flow of the Spirit, the more power for intercession. There is a divine orchestration when the Holy Spirit is allowed free rein in corporate worship—an orchestration that will harmonize and synchronize both the voices and the movements of the worshippers.

Preparation for battle

Have you noticed that there's an acceleration in the earth—of time and of events and of prophetic fulfillment? In these days there is an acceleration in both the things of God and in the galloping opposition to Him and His people. There are wars and rumors of wars in the natural, and there are spiritual battles in the heavenlies. Persecution of believers has begun in earnest and we know from God's end-time prophets and Jesus Himself that it will only increase as Jesus's return approaches (see e.g., Matthew 25), culminating in the final battle of Armageddon.

We are reassured that, when we begin to see these things come to pass, we are to lift up our heads and rejoice for our redemption draws nigh! (See Luke 21:28.) At the same time, we must constantly remind ourselves, as believers—and particularly those who feel specially called to intercession—not to march out onto the battlefield, even with our fellow soldiers "at our backs," with chinks in our armor. That can be very dangerous unless the chinks are not first closed up.

So how do we shore up the gaps and close up the chinks and strengthen the armor before engaging in battle? Even as we had to approach the holy place through repentance and cleansing, how much more before going to battle need we to come back to the cross, back to repentance, and back to worship—again and again, individually and corporately. I, for one, dare not don my armor over dirty garments.

So here in the context of corporate intercession, we need to stand reminded that, when we are entrusted with God's power, we need to have repented—however briefly— before venturing forth to battle. We need to remind ourselves that repentance is not just preparation for the holy of holies; repentance is also preparation for the battlefield.

Still, whether as an individual or as part of a corporate body, repentance is between you and God, under the "priesthood of all believers." You know what's on your hands; you know what's in your heart; you know what's escaped from your mouth; and God knows as well.

If you have been walking in the light and living a lifestyle of worship, it doesn't need to be a lengthy or agonizing session. He knows; you know; just repent and thank Him that He has forgiven you, even as (and this is important!) you have forgiven others. If this is the case, even just a brief time of repentance should suffice to ensure that your armor is adjusted and is securely in place and that beneath the armor you are clean, before going into corporate battle in intercession. If you earnestly confess, He instantly forgives…and forgets! And you are ready!

If, on the other hand, you personally are engaged in a habitual known sin, this should be repented of and dealt with in earnest *before* joining in with the intercessory army. Otherwise you will be a liability to your regiment as well as personally vulnerable to enemy attack. In this case, you do not belong on the battlefield. You need first to get right with God.

It is not His good pleasure to keep us down; He always wants to bring us higher. He wants us to join in with Him and He wants to join in with us—advancing the kingdom together with us by His Spirit. Still, before we can take and keep the gates of our city, we need clean hands and a pure heart. For both the throne and the battlefield, we need to approach together with a burning coal on our lips and in a true spirit of humility, reverence, and dependency on the King, our Commander-in-Chief.

H. WITH WHAT DO WE WORSHIP?

David was a man after God's own heart (see 1 Samuel 13:14; Acts 13:22). So *how* and *with what* did David worship?

Davidic worship

David's worship is first and foremost exemplified by the psalms that he composed and sang unto and about the Lord. Further, it was by the playing of David's harp that King Saul's troubled spirit was calmed and that the evil spirit departed from him. (See 1 Samuel 16:14–23.) It is not without significance that David became Saul's armor bearer! (See 1 Samuel 16:21.)

Now let's look at how and with what David worshipped:

> Make a joyful noise unto the LORD…
>
> —PSALM 100:1

Praise him upon the loud cymbals: praise him upon the high sounding cymbals. Let every thing that hath breath praise the LORD. Praise ye the LORD.
—PSALM 150:5–6; SEE ALSO PSALMS 33:3 AND 98:4

And David and all Israel played before God with all their might, and with singing, and with harps, and with psalteries, and with timbrels, and with cymbals, and with trumpets.
—1 CHRONICLES 13:8 (SEE ALSO 2 SAMUEL 6:5)

And David spake to the chief of the Levites to appoint their brethren to be the singers with instruments of musick, psalteries and harps and cymbals, sounding, by lifting up the voice with joy.
—1 CHRONICLES 15:16

Then what about the Levites, the priests (the intercessors *par excellence*)?

So the singers, Heman, Asaph, and Ethan, were appointed to sound with cymbals of brass…with shouting, and with sound of the cornet, and with trumpets, and with cymbals, making a noise with psalteries and harps.
—1 CHRONICLES 15:19, 28

And it came to pass, when the priests were come out of the holy place: (for all the priests that were present were sanctified, and did not then wait by course: Also the Levites which were the singers, all of them of Asaph, of Heman, of Jeduthun, with their sons and their brethren, being arrayed in white linen, having cymbals and psalteries and harps, stood at the east end of the altar, and with them an hundred and twenty priests sounding with trumpets:)

> It came even to pass, as the trumpeters and singers were as one, to make one sound to be heard in praising and thanking the Lord; and when they lifted up their voice with the trumpets and cymbals and instruments of musick, and praised the Lord, saying, For he is good; for his mercy endureth for ever: that then the house was filled with a cloud, even the house of the Lord; So that the priests could not stand to minister by reason of the cloud: for the glory of the Lord had filled the house of God.
>
> —2 Chronicles 5:11–14

> And all the congregation worshipped, and the singers sang, and the trumpeters sounded…
>
> —2 Chronicles 29:28

Note that when the priests came out of the *holy place*, the glory cloud came with them, as recorded again in the Book of Kings:

> And it came to pass, when the priests were come out of the holy place, that the cloud filled the house of the Lord…
>
> —1 Kings 8:10

The ideal accompaniment to our worship is of course the music of "live" anointed musicians, psalmists, and minstrels—in other words, anointed song writers, worship leaders, prophetic singers, and instrumentalists. They can lift us up into heavenly realms *even if* we haven't adequately prepared our hearts in worship beforehand (as we should). In today's culture our list of instruments will include the keyboard and the drum and cymbal sets, along with an endless variety of stringed instruments, from violins to electric guitars and more.

In large gatherings, with full worship teams, prophetic dancers, banners, and hundreds or thousands of worshippers, you will often be caught up effortlessly in the atmosphere of worship created by His presence even before the opening of the meeting, especially if intercessors have already broken through to the heavens in that place.

But what if we have no psalmists or players of instruments among us—in other words, if we have no "live" music?

Voice alone

Search the passages above for words that do not require "live" instrumentation: "make a joyful *noise*"; "...with *singing*";...with *shouting*"; "lifting up the *voice* with joy"; [they] praised the LORD, *saying*..." [the spoken word]. In fact, anything that has breath can praise and worship the Lord, with or without music, with or without instruments.

Even "lifting up the voice with joy" can be a spoken praise unto the Lord; it does not have to be in song. It can be simply "crying out with a loud voice," as with the Levites (the priestly praisers) below. Note also that the Levites here *spoke* ("*said*") their blessing and praise to the Lord.

> Then stood up upon the stairs, of the Levites...and cried with a loud voice unto the LORD their God. Then [other] Levites...*said*, Stand up and bless the LORD your God for ever and ever: and blessed be thy glorious name, which is exalted above all blessing and praise.
>
> —NEHEMIAH 9:4–5, EMPHASIS ADDED

This is in no way meant to decry or play down the use of musical accompaniment. Not in the least. Even though we can praise and worship without instruments, anointed music has always contributed to the atmosphere of heaven and thereby greatly enhanced the worship experience. This is simply to make us aware that we ought not to leave ourselves wholly reliant on instruments—large or small— or let the lack of same serve as an excuse for not coming together to worship. We can *always* find means to worship.

Small instruments

In addition to vocalizing our praise and worship, any worshipper can be an active participant in the music-making through the individual use of tambourines, cymbals, shakers, and other rhythmic handheld instruments of infinite form and variety. This can of course include the shofar, at appropriate times and in and by the Holy Spirit.

It is important with each of these instruments, but especially with the shofar, to be led into the timing and rhythms of the Holy Spirit. We have all had that experience of hearing a shofar blown at the wrong moment and shattering the anointing instead of elevating it. The effect is similar to hearing a "prophetic word" proceeding out of the "flesh" or out of a person's own spirit rather than by the Holy Spirit, and thereby bringing down a highly charged spiritual atmosphere. The shofar is a powerful instrument in the Spirit, and whoever blows it must be sensitive and responsive to the leading of the Holy Spirit.

Let the sounds and rhythms of the instruments and the trumpet call of the shofar be born in heaven and orchestrated from the throne; then let them be transmitted from there to the earth. Let the instruments accompany what God is doing in the heavenlies. There are times when the instruments should follow the worship rather than the worship following the instruments. It's all about flowing with the Holy Spirit.

Anointed CDs

In our day and age, live bands are not the only music to which we can join our singing, shouting, pronouncing, or making a joyful noise unto the Lord. In our "Breakthrough Worship" over Geneva, undeterred by the absence of musicians among us, we use the most anointed CDs I can gather up from anywhere on the planet—not to "lead" us *per se* (we invite the Holy Spirit to do that), but to lift us up, to support us, to help us shed the cares of the world that we may have come in with, so that we can better "enter in," and to help us not to be intimidated by the awkward sound of our own "naked" voices!

We occasionally begin by just singing out of our hearts, with no music accompaniment at all! This actually seems to particularly delight the heart of the Father, because when we do so, we can feel His distinct pleasure. He seems to find special enjoyment in the pure simplicity of our fresh childlike expressions of love and adoration, and we sense His paternal smile.

Needless to say, worship flows most freely when the anointing (His Holy Spirit) is present. But what is it that brings in the presence of the Holy Spirit? *The worship itself!* Even with pre-recorded music, the anointing flows from the music because the Holy Spirit was present when the music was recorded. This anointing can then be transmitted—at another time and in another place—to us, if we join in the same spirit of worship, with the common purpose of blessing Him. As long as our intent to bless and minister unto Him takes precedence over our desire to be touched and blessed by His presence, the Holy Spirit and His anointing will come.

I once ordered a worship CD that carried an extraordinary anointing when I first heard it, being, myself, already under the strong touch of the power of God on that occasion. When it arrived and I played it at home, I experienced virtually no anointing at all. Through this I discovered that the anointing on the music is related in no small part to our own place in the Spirit at any given time. In other words, the anointing on the music is partially dependent on the extent to which *we ourselves* are under the anointing (i.e., "in the Spirit"). I have indeed found that the more "in the Spirit" I am personally when listening to worship music—whether live or recorded—the more the sounds meeting my ear are anointed and the more I am taken yet higher and deeper into His presence!

The significance of our own spiritual state and sensitivity as we listen to worship music is again exemplified by another occasion where I put on a home-recorded cassette to accompany my prayer time and found the voice so grating to my ear that I simply had to turn it off. Yet at a later date, already in the midst of deep prayer, I felt prompted by the Holy Spirit to play that same cassette, only to find it so amazingly anointed that it took me still deeper and higher into the realms of glory!

Although the anointing on recorded music can certainly do much to lead us into God's holy presence, we should consider it no more than a starting point for our own worshipful ascent to the throne and realize that we ourselves play no small role in where it takes us.

Even when we make use of anointed CDs, for lack of a live psalmist, that is not the whole story. We should never become dependent on music created by others. Guess what: God knows that CD. He has heard it a thousand times and already knows it by heart. He wants something *fresh* from you. He wants to hear *your* voice! He wants to hear *your* "value added"! It's what you *add* to the worship song—*your voice* over and above the recording—that His ear is listening for.

The CD, as used for intercessory/breakthrough worship, is not meant for "easy listening." The aim is not to "soak" in the anointing of the CD or even to "sing along," however earnestly and sincerely. It should serve merely as support; as accompaniment; as a starting point; as a springboard to soar higher, through what we can *add* to it. The purpose is to refresh and further enhance the anointing from the CD by virtue of our own personal expressions of adoration.

At one all-night intercessory "watch" in Geneva, I had brought along my keyboard, which was open for anyone to play. (I don't play it well enough myself to lead by it, though it is my heart's desire to one day be able do so.) One newcomer approached the keyboard on the podium, installed herself, and began to play. It sounded as if she had never touched a piano or a keyboard before. She herself appeared to be quite captivated, but the sounds issuing forth were anything but harmonious.

What to do? I did not want to discourage this initiative that I had invited, so I let her go on playing. After all, I had welcomed anyone to do so. Not to be distracted from our intercession, we sang in the Spirit. The fact is, we had to sing louder, we had to pray more intensely, we had to push harder to come into the anointing.

This was in the days of our all-night prayer. She was our self-appointed musician that night—all night—9 p.m. to 6 a.m. That's nine hours! I have never fought so hard to bring in and hold on to the anointing. But in the morning, at 6 a.m., someone remarked: "Awesome! Glory!" Why? I suppose it's because we had to push harder to keep the anointing; we had to demand more of ourselves and give more! Result? More glory!

When you were a child, did you ever test that physical phenomenon where you stand in a doorway and push out with your arms on the doorjambs as hard as you can for as long as you can, then step forward out of the doorway and your arms just float upwards with virtually no effort on your part? That's how it seemed. We had to push so hard that we finished by just floating upward. Glory!

Generally speaking, however, which is better if you haven't access to truly anointed music—live music that isn't truly anointed, or CDs sung and recorded in the anointing? Well, I'll opt for the anointing every time, whatever way it comes. I will take an anointed CD over anything without the anointing, and then aim for the "value added."

The playlist

As a small intercessory worship group using CDs, I personally do not create a playlist in advance. I am not in any way implying that this is wrong or unspiritual; it can indeed be most effective and useful if you can get in the Spirit well before the worship gathering and receive the heart and flow of the Father for that night.

My own hesitation to prepare a "line-up" for CDs stems from the fact that I never know beforehand just where the Holy Spirit wants to go on any given worship night. Sometimes He leads us from worship into war, sometimes from war into worship, and occasionally He just takes us into His garden of delights and lets us dance or lie among the flowers and simply surprises us with an interlude of sweet repose in His awesome presence.

Having no playlist does place an additional burden on

the "leader" to be extra sensitive to where the Holy Spirit wants to go and what He wants to do next. Sometimes, while still in the midst of one worship song, I will be asking the Father: "What do You want to hear next; where do You want us to go next?"

One night, in response, the Holy Spirit impressed upon me to follow with a particular CD that I would not even normally play for the intercession night, for which I select only the most highly anointed CDs, even at the expense of curtailing variety. So my reaction was: "But Father, that one's not anointed enough. It's fine at home [while preparing a meal or washing the dishes]; but here, Father, it's not anointed enough for here!" I understood His still small voice to prompt me: "It is up to you to *add* the greater anointing."

Thus it was a challenge—a bit like with the self-styled keyboard player. The Holy Spirit wanted us to add more of His anointing to a CD that was a little less anointed so that we would have to reach higher. So I played the selection and, indeed, we did have to reach higher and pull harder to bring in His presence. But the anointing came; His presence came, and it was good—very good.

I have a large assortment of worship CDs and am always on the lookout for new and fresh anointed releases. Yet I tend to use the same couple of dozen week after week, because I am less after variety than I am after the anointing. I call that special anointing on the music the "golden edge." If that is not there, I care not for the words or the musical rendition. (I look for that same "golden edge" on the voices of live worship leaders, including on my own. No "golden edge," no glory realm!) As for the element of variety, it is the particular selections, the order of the selections, and our own fresh response and "value added" each week that, in itself, creates the diversity.

Incidentally, the absence of a playlist does not impact any potential projection of song texts onto a screen, since I personally prefer not to display the words to follow in any case. As breakthrough worshippers, we are not there to make music; we are there to make intercession. I prefer not to risk anchoring us in the earthly realm by virtue of having to use our natural senses even to read the spiritual words. This practice (or omission) would not necessarily be appropriate for all spiritual gatherings; we are talking here of small breakthrough worship sessions. We want nothing more than to enter in, lose ourselves in the Father and the Son, and catch the flow of the Holy Spirit.

Banners

Worship with banners has thus far only been mentioned in passing, yet a whole book could be written about the use of banners in praise and worship—the different forms (from simple to ceremonial/processional), the different colors, the different movements. It is not necessary to enter into great detail here. Like all other aspects of true worship, the important thing is to be led by the Spirit. It is often more meaningful to learn by doing rather than to do by learning.

Suffice it to say that worship banners—created and/or waved under the inspiration of the Holy Spirit—can both carry and impart a palpable anointing. If you have ever been present where heavily embroidered and richly adorned banners have been processed down the aisle in a service, or simply placed on view to bless the beholder, you will undoubtedly have experienced the weight of glory that they can emit.

Then there are the lighter, wavable—characteristically silk—banners that are designed for movement and tend to play a greater role in active worship than the heavy ceremonial ones. These should reflect the movement and mood or purposes of what the Holy Spirit is doing or saying at any given point in time. They are really only anointed when the one bearing them or waving them is doing so by the Spirit of God. Thus banners should be treated with sensitivity and respect as an instrument of worship and potential carrier of the anointing.

You may discover charts of colors and their spiritual meanings, as relates to banners, but note that colors are not rigidly assigned meanings in the Bible. I personally never consulted a list of colors, but would simply pick up banners in the course of worship whose colors for me had an association with where the Holy Spirit seemed to be taking us at that particular moment.

In our Geneva group, we began with a mere six small banners—in hues of purple, violet, and magenta—that had been given to me expressly for Geneva as I left Washington DC for my UN posting. At that time, I had never used banners in worship. But in various gatherings in DC I had witnessed a petite but powerful African American sister, always dressed in black from head to toe—hat to heels—who, when she resolutely, if not to say defiantly, marched across the front with those banners, caused something to happen in the atmosphere! She it was who offered me these six small banners—most likely made by her own hand—to take along to Geneva, for the nations.

Some time after eventually having started up the

worship nights there, I began to have a spiritual hunger for larger banners—I mean *really big banners*—in anticipation of the ultimate realization of my vision for a "24/7" intercessory worship center in Switzerland, with oh-so-high ceilings and volumes of space!

My original and persistent desire was for one large red and one large white banner. Quite subconsciously, I suppose the red represented to me the blood of Jesus that washes white as snow, and the white, the resultant snow/purity/holiness. All I knew was, my spirit yearned for large banners in those two colors. I had already started collecting full-sized flags of nations for our worship nights, also with the same long-term vision in view.

At last one day—the final day of a huge "*Levitenkamp*" ("Levite camp") held in Switzerland—just before leaving, I entered an enormous tent filled with many alluring items for purchase and came upon an abundant source of banners of all colors, shapes, and sizes. My heart leapt, and I immediately seized upon two large banners in my two coveted colors.

But that didn't satisfy me. I next sought out a blue banner, which I associated with priesthood, prophecy, and peace. Then that would certainly need to be accompanied by a purple banner, which I associated with kingship and majesty. I just couldn't leave that big tent without adding a yellow banner, which to me represented joy and praise. But then I absolutely had to have an orange banner for holy fire, for the Lion of the Tribe of Judah and for glory. And of course we could not be left without gold, which to me represented God's kingdom riches and His most precious substance, from Genesis to Revelation, also victory. Still, the gold would be incomplete without the company of silver, similarly representing God's riches, and—as I perceived it—faith.

Before finally departing from that place, I stood with my arms clutched around eight large banners, and was then awarded one additional banner, offered as a gift by the banner man. It was copper, which to me represented justice and seemed a most appropriate (even prophetic) addition for an international lawyer. My collection was complete, and I was at last satisfied.

Now, my interpretation and attribution of these colors need not be the same as yours. I never researched their "accepted" symbolism. This is simply what they basically represent to me personally, without much thought or analysis. Let yourself be led by what the various colors might suggest to you personally. You are also likely to discover that, as you are led to pick up one banner or another, in the flow of worship, you may begin to combine colors, such as:

- purple and gold—kingship, royalty, majesty;

- silver and gold—His riches, abundance;

- silver and white—wedding, marriage, bride and Bridegroom;

- red and white—the blood of the Lamb, holiness and purity;

- blue and purple—kings and priests;

- orange and red—holy fire, warfare;

- yellow and orange—joy, praise, celebration.

You will surely make your own associations and combinations that are equally meaningful. There are no rules here. The Lord is attentive to your heart of worship, and He will know your intent.

In addition, there are beautiful banners that were created to appear as flames of fire; or, for example, as a rainbow; or that depict an actual image of a lion, a lamb, a dove, or other spiritually meaningful symbol. The possibilities are infinite. You may even be inspired to create some banners of your own design.

National flags can also effectively be displayed and/or waved, as appropriate, especially that of Israel and/or that of your own country or of another nation that God has laid on your heart, as well as one(s) that your group is targeting specially on a given worship night. Banners and national flags are, after all, both used to good effect in real warfare, as often depicted in the Scriptures, so are therefore perfectly suited to warfare worship.

As the Holy Spirit is present and allowed to lead, you may well notice, as you pick up certain banners with colors that speak to you out of the words being sung or prophesied, that another or several other worshippers have picked up the same colors. You may even find that you are spontaneously moving in sync with the movements of others, as together you flow in the tempo and "mood" that has been created by the music and the corresponding worship. You have picked up on the same mind and flow of the Spirit. Think of the spiritual authority available to you when you are at one in the Spirit. And when the whole troop is in harmony by the Spirit, what intercessory power!

As you worship with banners, you may find yourself performing simple prophetic acts. In our Geneva group, without premeditation, we began to lay down, hang up, or prop against one another—spontaneously, in meaningful patterns—banners that we had just finished wielding or waving during a given song or group of songs.

For example, a certain worshipper, after using, say, a banner of fire, might finish by laying that fire banner beside, beneath, or overlapping a flag of a nation that has been prayed over for revival. Or a similar juxtaposition might occur with a rainbow banner, or a Lion of Judah banner, in relation to, for example, the flag of Israel. In this way, a prophetic representation would begin to emerge that was, in a sense, a symbolic record of the night's intercession. Thus by the end of the night, we would have before our eyes and before the altar a magnificent cohesive worship "offering," representing the stream and direction of our worship throughout that night.

The result was usually quite magnificent and projected an anointing of its own, beyond that of the individual banners themselves—refreshingly unique each time. This cannot and should not be planned or "programmed." While I longed to capture these awesome worship "monuments" on camera at the end of the night, I was afraid that we might begin to build our "altar" of worship with the end photo in mind, rather than purely spontaneously by the Spirit. Consequently, there is no permanent record of these symbolic prophetic "altars" emanating from the nights of worship, but I believe they are forever recorded in heaven.

So once again, the important thing is to be led by the Holy Spirit. This is not to suggest that it is unspiritual to practice different moves with your banners when you are on your own, or even collectively with others. Many of us have experienced the spiritual impact of well-rehearsed and synchronized banners. But, whether rehearsed or spontaneous, the movements of the banners in the worship setting should enhance the atmosphere of worship, in concert with the music.

Banners may be made available for all in the group to share, but a certain "banner etiquette" should be observed, because these are not to be regarded as mere "props" but as articles of worship—temple instruments—and should be respected as such. They develop a certain sanctity, through their use in worship, that should not be violated.

I once left behind our original six precious hand-crafted banners at the church where we first began. As soon as I realized this, I felt a sword go through my spirit with the thought that they could end up some place where they might be "innocently" defiled by persons unfamiliar with banners and their sacred use. It transpired that the banners had been safely rescued by someone else from the worship group itself. But my sense of alarm and surprisingly strong protective instinct, pending their recovery, served to heighten my awareness of the real spiritual worth of these "temple instruments."

Banners can become very personal and quite sacrosanct to the individual worshipper who has carried them before the very throne of God in worship. A proper sensitivity toward these "temple instruments" dictates that personally owned banners should not be used by others without their first obtaining the express consent of the person to whom they belong. It is always preferable to have your own collection of banners. You will undoubtedly find that you have a similar protective instinct about them as regards preserving their sanctity for worship.

In sum, banners carry a singular anointing—both to lead into worship and to lead into battle. They should enrich the intercessory worship experience of all who are present—both those who wield them and those who simply behold them.

> Lift ye up a banner upon the high mountain, exalt the voice unto them, shake the hand, that they may go into the gates of the nobles.
>
> —ISAIAH 13:2

SOME IMPORTANT PRACTICAL ASPECTS IN CORPORATE WORSHIP

ALLOW ME TO share some practical aspects of corporate worship, out of my own experience, that have played a significant role in the enrichment of our worship nights and that can help in "entering into" and maintaining the anointing.

No one need absorb all the following observations at one time; but once you have tucked some of these thoughts into your conscious or subconscious mind, you will discover a new awareness of what is right for your particular situation and worship environment. The following pointers should simply support your worship experience and hopefully enhance that experience for you and for all present. You need only appropriate those that you find applicable to your situation, digest them, then forget about them and enjoy your breakthrough worship!

You may find that some of what you absorb from these few pages that follow will imperceptibly become a part of your own worship experience, if they aren't already. You will also not only have your own testimonies to add to what is shared here but will go on to discover altogether new ways to honor your King and perhaps write your own book for the benefit of the rest of us.

Or you may simply find yourself more open and sensitive to things that you perhaps overlooked up until now, that can unwittingly compromise the anointing—not only for you personally, but for the other worshippers as well. The possibilities open for learning by experience are limitless. We all learn by stepping out and doing, as well as by sharing with others what we have discovered.

A. Physical Posture in Worship

What does posture have to do with worship? Surely this goes too far. God accepts us as we are and whatever way we come to Him! This is of course true. Nonetheless, I invite you at least to consider the illustrative[*] Scriptures below from the Old Testament.

The relevant Scriptures

> And the man *bowed down his head, and worshipped* the LORD.
> —GENESIS 24:26, EMPHASIS ADDED

> And it came to pass, that, when Abraham's servant heard their words, he *worshipped* the LORD, *bowing himself to the earth.*
> —GENESIS 24:52, EMPHASIS ADDED

> And Jehoshaphat *bowed his head with his face to the ground:* and all Judah and the inhabitants of Jerusalem *fell before the Lord, worshipping* the LORD.
> —2 CHRONICLES 20:18, EMPHASIS ADDED

---

[*] For a full list of such Scriptures see Appendix II.

And he said, Nay; but as captain of the host of the
Lord am I now come. And Joshua *fell on his face to
the earth, and did worship...*
>   —JOSHUA 5:14, EMPHASIS ADDED

Then Job arose, and rent his mantle, and shaved
his head, and *fell down upon the ground, and
worshipped...*
>   —JOB 1:20, EMPHASIS ADDED

...and from the New Testament:

And when they [the wise men] were come into the
house, they saw the young child with Mary his
mother, and *fell down, and worshipped him.*
>   —MATTHEW 2:11, EMPHASIS ADDED

And the four beasts said, Amen. And the four and
twenty elders fell down and worshipped him that
liveth for ever and ever.
>   —REVELATION 5:14, EMPHASIS ADDED

And the four and twenty elders, which sat before
God on their seats, *fell upon their faces, and worshipped God...*
>   —REVELATION 11:16, EMPHASIS ADDED

In both Old and New Testaments, nearly all the
Scriptures say "and they fell [down upon the ground
/ upon their faces / before the Lord / before the throne]
and worshipped", or they "bowed [down / themselves /
their heads] [to the earth / faces to the ground] and worshipped." Actually only one passage adds kneeling:

> O come, let us *worship and bow down*: let us *kneel before the Lord* our maker.
>
> —PSALM 95:6, EMPHASIS ADDED

It may be of interest to note that, in the Old Testament, there are twice as many references to "bowing down" as there are to "falling down" to worship, while in the New Testament, *every* reference is to "falling down" (before the Lord / the Lamb / the throne). "Bowing down" would seem to indicate a rather controlled (albeit sincere) reverence of Jehovah God, while "falling down" would suggest being suddenly overcome by the Spirit of God or by Jesus's holy presence, and dropping in awe at His feet.

The Old Testament believers bowed in reverence to a holy God, with the Spirit of God coming and going on His prophets and priests. When the New Testament believers suddenly found themselves in the very presence of Jesus, they could only respond by falling at His feet.

"Feet" and "footstool" are indeed mentioned specifically in a few of the New Testament references, as well as the Old:

> And as they went to tell his disciples, behold, Jesus met them, saying, All hail. And they came *and held him by the feet, and worshipped him.*
>
> —MATTHEW 28:9, EMPHASIS ADDED

> …behold, I will make them to come and *worship before thy feet*, and to know that I have loved thee.
>
> —REVELATION 3:9, EMPHASIS ADDED

> Exalt ye the LORD our God, and *worship at his footstool*; for he is holy.
>
> —PSALM 99:5, EMPHASIS ADDED

> We will go into his tabernacles: we will *worship at his footstool.*
>
> —Psalm 132:7, emphasis added

Our physical response to His presence

As noted earlier, in connection with the spiritual as distinct from the physical location of God's throne, we can say here that wherever we come to Jesus's feet and fall down to worship Him, that, spiritually, is His "footstool" (or His throne). If Jesus were standing bodily right before me, as with those who lived in His time, I too would surely fall at His feet. Even now, we can fall at His feet in His very presence, as He may actually be there in person in the room.

I may otherwise find myself on my knees or bowed down on the floor. The deeper the worship and the stronger His presence, the more I am liable to find myself bending/bowing lower—not infrequently until I am flat out prostrate, face down on the floor, arms outstretched.

At the same time, despite all the above Old and New Testament Scriptures, if I am worshipping Him where He now sits, above on His heavenly throne, at the right hand of God the Father, I am more inclined to raise my head and my hands toward heaven, where He is enthroned. So I mostly instinctively begin my worship with my face turned upward and my hands raised high. And when the spirit of intercession for the nations comes, I am up on my feet!

There is an Old Testament passage where, when Moses entered the tabernacle in the desert and the "cloudy pillar" descended, the people did *not bow down*; they *rose up* at the door of the tent and worshipped.

> And all the people saw the cloudy pillar stand at the tabernacle door: and all the people *rose up* and worshipped, every man in his tent door.
>
> —EXODUS 33:10, EMPHASIS ADDED

We have already seen how the Levites (priests) exhorted the children of Israel to:

> *Stand up and bless the Lord your God* for ever and ever: and blessed be thy glorious name, which is exalted above all blessing and praise.
>
> —NEHEMIAH 9:5, EMPHASIS ADDED

And in another Old Testament passage, in Ezekiel, during certain feast days, the prince worshipped at the *gate*.

> And *the prince shall enter by the way of the porch of that gate* without, and shall *stand by the post of the gate*, and the priests shall prepare his burnt offering and his peace offerings, and he shall *worship at the threshold of the gate*: then he shall go forth; but the gate shall not be shut until the evening. *Likewise the people of the land shall worship at the door of this gate* before the LORD in the sabbaths and in the new moons.
>
> —EZEKIEL 46:2–3, EMPHASIS ADDED

In intercessory worship, when I want to "take the gates," I personally find myself much more on my feet than on my face, at least until the battle is done. This is because we are interceding for nations, and in order to "take the gates," we need to set a watch, as sentries. It is the duty of sentries to stand at the gates.

Being on our feet also helps us to be ready to adjust our armor, or to grab up a banner, or to join in a battle or victory march, or to sound the shofar, or even to dance before the Lord like David. For such things, we should be standing, alert and at attention, even though we may ultimately end up on our face.

The deeper worship—the falling down or lying prostrate before Him—normally comes after the victory is won, following the sense of great joy and jubilation that generally accompanies the breakthrough. Sometimes we find that after a hard fought battle, He leads us all together into green pastures and beside still waters (see Psalm 23:2). It is then that I most often find myself prostrate, falling down before Him to worship Him, emptied of my own strength and ready to be restored by His.

Posture to avoid

I personally find that, over the course of a Breakthrough Worship night, I may assume a number of different positions. I am not even mindful of this; it is an unconscious response. But I have found that one position to be avoided above all in intercessory (*active* as opposed to *passive*) worship is sitting down (unless you have a physical ailment that demands it). My experience has been that the leader must never sit down. If the leader sits down, it's a little like Moses letting down his arms; the intercessory anointing drops dramatically. As you will recall, whenever Moses lifted up his hands, Israel prevailed in battle over the enemy; but when he let down his arms, Israel would begin to lose the battle (see Exodus 17:11).

This applies to more than the leader, especially where small groups are concerned. While there is no single "correct" position for breakthrough praise and worship, I have never seen anyone—and that includes myself—able to effectively break through in praise or worship seated comfortably in a pew. It would be hard for me to imagine even uttering a real shout while sitting down. This does not mean you cannot *worship* seated quietly in a pew. You can *always* worship. I am talking here about *breakthrough* intercessory worship.

When I am leading, I can physically feel a weightiness and a shift in the spirit when someone in the room sits down. I can sense when that person disengages from active worship. There is a distinct drop in the anointing. If I myself, as "leader," even partially disengage while searching for a certain musical selection without locating it at once, I can feel the anointing in the room begin to recede. This just demonstrates the force of unity and the vital role played by each individual worshipper corporately, especially in a small group.

For a person who is not leading, sitting down will not affect the whole group *as severely* as if the leader sits down. But that person should be aware that it can still impact the spiritual dynamic in the room and that it can affect the level of anointing for everyone present (in a small group) as well as for that worshipper him/herself. The effect on the atmosphere of worship is of course less in a huge convocation, where the individual is an infinitesimal part of the whole and can go virtually unnoticed, while his/her "place" is carried unknowingly by the others, who unconsciously fill in the ranks.

Where there is good cause, of course there is no condemnation. If there is a physical impediment, where you need to sit, you will just have to stand, leap, and dance in the Spirit! This is even a greater challenge, so might even reap a greater reward. I have seen people "dance" in a wheelchair.

If you are tired, there is a safer place for you to be

refreshed than on the battlefield, so go and take your rest. Father will carry you in His loving arms. If you should want to remain with the troops, it is better to lie prone than to sit. But if you are fit, able-bodied, and unconstrained, get on your feet and move! This is breakthrough worship!

Although worship is very personal and individual, in corporate worship, as noted earlier, there is a special orchestration from heaven. The worshippers will ideally be in the "same place" at the same time, spiritually, if they are all following the Holy Spirit. There may even come a "holy hush" that settles upon everyone when all are in unity and particularly sensitive to the Spirit. You feel breathless, and no one dares move. Jesus has come into the room and is moving about in your midst.

Summing up

Whatever your physical position in worship at any given moment, it should reflect an attitude of awe and respect toward our Maker and Redeemer and should allow freedom of expression and motion. The Holy Spirit is a Spirit in motion. We each need to be a malleable vessel and one that is ready to receive God's power to flow through us and to motivate us, attentive at all times and submissive to the movements of the Holy Spirit.

B. Dressing for the Throne Room

I know this may cause a ripple. Of course we can worship no matter how we are dressed; and we certainly can dress in some pretty amazing ways to come before the throne of God; and no one seems to mind. All reverent and passionate worshippers are welcome at the throne. But did you ever notice this passage in which the clothing of the priestly (i.e., intercessory) praisers and worshippers is described?

Priestly attire

> And it came to pass, when the *priests* were come out
> of the *holy place*:…being *arrayed in white linen*…
> —2 CHRONICLES 5:11–12, EMPHASIS ADDED

Or 2 Chronicles 20:21:

> …when he had taken counsel with the people, he
> appointed those who were to *sing* to the LORD and
> *praise* him *in holy attire*…
> —ESV, EMPHASIS ADDED

Or Ezekiel 42:14:

> When the *priests* enter therein, then shall they not
> go out of the holy place into the [outer] court, but
> there they shall *lay their garments wherein they
> minister*; for they are *holy*; and shall put on other
> garments…(emphasis added).

Or Exodus 35:19:

> The *cloths of service*, to do service *in the holy place*,
> the holy garments for Aaron the *priest*, and the gar-
> ments of his sons, *to minister in the priest's office*
> (emphasis added).

Or Leviticus 16:23:

> And *Aaron* shall come into the tabernacle of the
> congregation, and shall put off *the linen garments*,

which he put on when he went *into the holy place*, and shall leave them there…(emphasis added).

Or 2 Samuel 12:20:

Then *David* arose from the earth, and washed, and anointed himself, and *changed his apparel*, and came into the house of the LORD, and *worshipped*…(emphasis added).

This of course does not mean that we all have to arrive at our worship gatherings wearing white linen or other "holy attire" or special ministering garments. As New Testament believers, we do not necessarily try to imitate in every respect the Old Testament priests, nor—other than as intercessors—do we stand between the holy place and the people. Still, it should cause us to stop and reflect. Think about it. It was important enough to be recorded in God's Word. We then, as priestly intercessors, should not altogether dismiss these Scriptures out of hand.

God is always pleased at our praise and worship if we offer up an acceptable "sacrifice" of praise and an acceptable offering of worship to Him. But we might also give some consideration to the respect that we owe the Almighty God of the Universe—the Alpha and Omega, the only true God and our Savior Jesus Christ—and at least consider clothing ourselves with this in mind.

Consider Psalm 96:9:

O worship the LORD in the beauty of holiness: fear [show respect] before him, all the earth.

Whether or not we dress in white linen or in holy attire, we will want to dress modestly, in a way that will not distract or hinder in any way our fellow worshippers.

In His image

You may even find that the Lord Himself will "dress you" prophetically for certain occasions, in colors of His own choosing, for reasons perhaps known only to Him, or possibly revealed to you by His Spirit. The first time I became consciously aware of this was one night at an intercessory prayer conference where I had distinctly sensed the Lord wanted me to wear red, and had therefore dressed accordingly. At some point in the evening I suddenly noticed that an unusual number of other women were also wearing red. I was struck by this and felt as if we had all been tuned in to the same instructions and were all unwittingly taking part in something prophetically profound.

On certain occasions I directly ask Father beforehand what He would like me to wear, according to what "image" He would like me to convey in a given circumstance in order to best represent Him or best carry out His purposes. It may be for a diplomatic function or it may be for a church function. It matters not. I represent Him at every occasion.

I do not want to blow this out of proportion but only to raise an awareness. The intent here is simply to show that the Holy Spirit is involved even in the smallest detail of our spiritual lives and that we should be aware that He is not totally indifferent to our attire, even in worship.

Summing up

To sum up, then, God will accept us and rejoice in us whatever way we come, but He is pleased when we take extra care to show honor and reverence to Him. He is blessed when we desire and seek to please Him. God's people, the Jews, know how to show respect to the Holy One of Israel, by their garments of prayer as well as by their posture of prayer. To them it is not a matter of indifference. We could perhaps learn something from our Jewish brothers and sisters.

C. Things That Hinder the Anointing[*]

Arriving late

To achieve the vital ingredient of unity in corporate worship and to show respect for the King, the worshippers should make every effort to arrive on time. We need to flow as one body in intercession, and it makes such a difference, in getting to the throne, when we all climb the holy hill together. We get so much higher and go so much deeper, so much faster.

We are all aware that the only unpardonable sin is against the Holy Spirit, and we are also exhorted not to grieve Him. When we really think about it, why indeed should the Holy Spirit lead us into the very holy of holies, truly into the awesome sanctity of the King's chambers, when some of the invited guests are still arriving in the outer court, and some have not yet washed their hands or changed their garments?

Our heavenly Father is amazingly tolerant and shows us more grace than we reasonably deserve. We expect Him to give us His best wine, His most precious gems, His most intimate touch, yet we so often fail to walk in the reverential fear of the Lord. We have often neglected to show Him the honor and awe-filled respect that is due Him, and we

---

* See also Appendix I

are all too frequently casual about when we arrive to keep our appointments with Him.

If you had an invitation to visit the queen of England at Buckingham Palace, or, say, the president of the United States in the Oval Office of the White House, or the pope at the Vatican, would you simply arrive at your convenience? I expect you would do all in your power even to arrive early, so as not to risk being one moment late. Should we be more casual with an appointment with the King of kings?

Well, you might argue that our appointment is not exactly with the King of kings but is merely with the worship group, so it's really not so important. But it is not only about keeping an appointment—or not—with the King Himself, but it is equally about joining with others at the appointed time to undertake the King's business together.

If we are to err in our approach to the King, let us rather err on the side of more reverence than on the side of more familiarity. This includes respect for not only the Godhead Himself but also for our fellow worshippers.

All have gathered to accomplish something together for the kingdom and must come into unity to do so. Therefore we need—as much as is possible—to be in the same place in the Spirit as we climb the holy hill or enter the temple gates and proceed toward the inner court together. Once we have started up the mountain or are headed for the inner court, there should not be the slightest interference—however discreet an entrance—in the midst of His awesome outpouring of Himself to accomplish His kingdom business.

I have been confronted in this regard with the argument that late or *ad hoc* arrival should not be an issue, in that it occurs every Sunday morning in churches everywhere, as well as in Christian meetings and conferences, with no apparent disruption. But we are not talking about large assemblies here; we are talking about small groups of dedicated, focused intercessors. The smaller the group, the more critical it is to arrive on time and to start off together.

There is a significant difference between arriving late amidst hundreds or thousands of churchgoers or conference attendees and arriving late to a small group of intercessory worshippers. If two people walk in late to a gathering of, say, three hundred congregants, they represent .0066666666667 percent of the assembly. They are therefore unlikely to disrupt the service, which may well not even have intercessory worship anywhere on the program. If, on the other hand, two people walk in late to a gathering of twenty intercessory worshippers, they constitute 10 percent of the company which, furthermore, may already be moving in effectual intercession, this being their sole and singular purpose in being there. The late entrance is very likely to hinder the flow. If there were to be an even smaller group of, say, six intercessory worshippers, the two latecomers would constitute *one third* of the body present. Now, that is interruptive.

Ideally, all should be moving with the Holy Spirit in single-minded, single-hearted total absorption in the Lord God and His program together from the start. Because if you're up here in the Spirit, and someone comes in the door—they've just been shopping; they bought the wrong size; somebody stole their wallet; somebody almost hit their car—and they come in, and they bring all that on in with them, they are not going to be in the flow of the Spirit. Moreover, they also bring with them the spirits of frustration and anger that most likely are at that moment still clinging to them.

And here we are—the rest of us—part way up the mountain, and we have to come down. We don't *want* to come down, but that disruption brings us down, and we have to try to bring this person up—if we can—and this person is laden down. They won't go up on their own; we have to carry them up; and they are very, very heavy.

Not only can even the fact of a door opening and the rustling of coats and other items in small quarters interfere with the progressive journey up the hill or through the outer to the inner courts, but those latecomers will normally find it harder themselves to "enter in" or to get "in step" with the rest. This can potentially cause the group as a whole to "lose ground," or even to woefully or willfully come back down the mountain—or back out of the inner court—to pick up the latecomers and try to bring them along up, or on in. That hinders everyone's progression, especially with a small number, which means that this in turn can compromise the entire objective of the night's intercessory worship.

Most of us simply do not realize what a difference it makes, not only to the Holy Spirit, who wholly merits respect, but, consequently, to what level of His anointing and presence *we ourselves* will be able to climb, as intercessors. The interruption of latecomers affects the intensity of the holy visitation for each of us who have come to give honor to the Father and to the Son, to minister unto Him (plural), by the Spirit, and to make effectual intercession.

On rare occasions, when arriving late is unanticipated and unavoidable, don't turn back! The disruption can be somewhat diminished if the latecomer is already "in the Spirit" upon arrival. This comes through having, for example, worshipped in the car, or enveloped him/herself in an atmosphere of worship in some way, en route. He or she can then slip in fairly unobtrusively and join in with relative ease. The alternative of staying away would only lend a victory to the enemy. You are loved and your presence is desired!

So ideally, you want to start together, climb together, stay together. Once you start out, if you seem to be tripping and stumbling, whatever, just keep together. He is watching; the angels are rooting for you—cheering you on. You will be all the stronger when you break through, like the butterfly gaining vital strength for life by having to break through the hard walls of the cocoon. You will be stronger, even as you prevail!

Distracting movement

Many types of movement—banners, dance, small instruments, marching, etc.—are an exhilarating and marvelous part of praise and worship which also pleases God and enhances the intercession. Think how David's dance pleased God, even though there were those to whom it looked excessive, "over the top," and foolish (see 2 Samuel 6:14–16, 20–23).

At the same time, *inappropriate* movement / movement "in the flesh" rather than "in the Spirit," at high points in intimate worship, can destroy the most sacred of moments in God's presence, especially in a small group, for reasons referred to above.

Let me give an example, because it's not always so apparent: In the middle of a worship evening where CDs are being used, someone particularly likes a piece of music playing at that moment. They understandably want to know what it is and walk across the room to look at the CD cover. Even though for an innocent and sincere motive, they have necessarily had to re-enter the "realm of the flesh" to check out the CD. This alone can affect the level of anointing in the room, because someone has stepped out of the spiritual realm and entered into the natural realm, thus disturbing the highly charged spiritual atmosphere. The fine-tuned sanctity is compromised. We are talking here again of small groups. The very movement "in the flesh" interferes with the sensitive spirit of worship that is present and flowing in the room.

Also in the midst of worship, the act of going out—even just to the kitchen for, say, a coffee or refreshment, which involves opening doors and potentially leaving them ajar—causes a distraction from the worship and can result in a breach of the anointing in the room, especially when there is noise and talking on the other side of the door. If worshippers are going in and out, one or several at a time, *all* who are present are likely to be affected. We often don't realize to what extent we are dishonoring (and thus grieving) the Object of our worship, and how much we are disturbing the rarefied atmosphere of the worship and intercession.

I am persuaded that, even in our most earnest efforts to please Him, we "innocently" and unwittingly take His Holy Spirit far too lightly. He so longs to pour out more, to pull us still closer, to bring us still higher, to overwhelm us still more totally.

"Horizontal" vs "vertical" communication

I have saved this one for the *last* because it is almost certainly the *first* in importance. While the other distractions have to do with the movement of our bodies, this one has to do with the movement of our tongues!

...If any man offend not in word, the same is a perfect man, and able also to bridle the whole body...the tongue is a little member, and boasteth great things. Behold, how great a matter a little fire kindleth! And the tongue is a fire, a world of iniquity: so is the tongue among our members, that it defileth the whole body, and setteth on fire the course of nature; and it is set on fire of hell...the tongue can no man tame; it is an unruly evil, full of deadly poison.

—JAMES 3:2, 5–6, 8

I am sure, dear reader, that this does not describe your tongue, which has been purged with a coal of fire. But even if this Scripture overstates the case here, let us nonetheless consider the following, since, when we enter the "special place," we are entering the highly sensitive throne zone.

When we first enter the place of meeting and begin to interact and briefly fellowship with one another prior to the start of worship, we must be careful not to greet one another by sharing what an awful day we've had, or what so-and-so said or did, or any negative communication whatsoever. Such talk defiles the atmosphere and invites the entrance of corresponding spirits.

Similarly, our intercessory worship gathering is not the place to discuss unholy things or other "gods," even in a negative sense. That includes Freemasonry, Satan, cults, demonic activity, or even some material thing that we might have made a "god" in our life. This attracts those spirits to enter our place of worship and similarly pollutes the environment. We are there to focus on our magnificent Maker and our Savior Bridegroom alone. We need to keep the atmosphere clear of all unclean and hindering spirits.

> Finally, brethren, whatsoever things are true, what-
> soever things are honest, whatsoever things are
> just, whatsoever things are pure, whatsoever things
> are lovely, whatsoever things are of good report; if
> there be any virtue, and if there be any praise, think
> on these things. Those things, which ye have both
> learned, and received, and heard, and seen in me,
> do: and the God of peace shall be with you.
>
> —PHILIPPIANS 4:8–9

Apart from the above admonitions, once the worship has begun, this final "rule" is as simple as it is critical: *No talking. NO talking.*

If you *absolutely* need to communicate something to someone, you should both *quietly* slip out of the room, taking special care to try not to break the anointing of worship. But remember that even the door opening can affect the level of the anointing, so communication should be reserved for emergencies only. Talking—even whispering; indeed, any "horizontal" communication— can bring down the anointing and affect the spiritual atmosphere for everyone. This is particularly true for a small group.

So at this point there should be no communication whatsoever *among* the worshippers—this includes gestures to one another and eye contact—or *by* the worshippers with others *outside* the place of worship. This means no cell phone use, no texting, no messaging…

We are there solely to minister unto Him and to worship Him until we are inundated by His presence and arrive at His throne—whether up the mountain or into the holy place. Our focus must be resolutely fixed on Him as we rise on wings like eagles, to the glory realm. Whether we are allowed to simply stand in the glory as He pours out the substance of our worship as intercession, or whether He calls us to follow Him into battle for a glorious victory, we must leave our earthly communications behind if we are truly to make it into the glory realm.

Summing up

God Almighty is ever so holy, so very, very pure and holy. To receive our worship, however deficient it is, He wants to come down in such measure that we can scarcely breathe, in *His glory*—that even to *move* (if indeed possible) would seem an insensitivity and sacrilege. For this level of blessing, we must not lose our reverential fear of the one true God, Jehovah, Lord God of the universe, Almighty King, Creator and Defender, Alpha and Omega, the Beginning and the End!

CONCLUSION

WE ALL ARE desirous of "going higher"! I, for one, am not satisfied. There is more—much more! We want to go higher, we want to go deeper. And you know, just like a building, if we try to go too high without going deep, we're going to come down. But the deeper we go, the higher we can build and the higher we can ascend the mountain of the Lord.

There will always be a call and a desire to go deeper yet and higher still. There are no limits in God, and we can go there together if we approach in unity. We want to draw near lovingly and joyously but with utmost respect and reverence—honoring the Father's and the Son's awesome majesty and the Holy Spirit's extreme sensitivity—when venturing to tread in the holiest of holies! It is all about *Him. He* is all that matters. And there is *more, much more,* praise His Holy name!

So let us keep moving and climbing together until that glorious day when the Bridegroom comes in all His splendor. He will come when the bride has prepared herself. He will come when the whole of creation groans and travails and cries out to Him: "Come!" He will come when the Spirit and the bride say "Come"!

I believe that the primary way for the bride to prepare

herself in this measure is through unfettered praise and worship, ushering in the glory realm and ultimately ushering in King Jesus, the "King of glory" (Ps. 24:10)!

Indeed, it has long been my sense that the Rapture of the Church[*] will take place at a moment in time when true believers everywhere will be in high praise and all-consuming worship. This would be orchestrated by God and not by man, who would in fact not even be aware that this is happening simultaneously around the globe. In this scenario, worshippers everywhere will be so lost in the Spirit—will be in such a place of unity and glory—that they will not even be conscious of the fact that they are rising in the air to meet the Object of their worship. All eyes will be upon Him, Jesus Christ the Bridegroom King! So let us persevere in breakthrough worship until He comes.

Maranatha! Amen.

---

[*]   See generally, Cynthia D. Wallace, *Don't Miss the Rapture: A Scriptural Re-Examination of the End-Time Scenario* (Lake Mary, FL: Creation House, 2011).

SOME WORSHIP GROUP PROTOCOL

THE FOLLOWING ARE important guidelines, but they are not meant to get in the way of your freedom of worship. They should become part and parcel of your worship experience and serve to enhance that experience for you and for all present. Be aware of them, absorb them, appropriate them, then forget them and enjoy your breakthrough worship!

- **Do not** enter the place of worship and greet others by sharing what an awful day you've had. This pollutes the atmosphere and invites the entrance of corresponding spirits. You usher those unclean spirits into the worship place and it can be very hard work for the worship leader to restore and maintain the level of anointing needed for breakthrough worship.

- **Do not** speak of other "gods" or unholy things—that includes Freemasonry, Satan, cults, demonic activity, or even some material thing that you have made a "god" in your life. This invites those spirits to enter

your place of worship and defile the sur-
roundings. We are there to focus on our
magnificent God and our Savior Bridegroom
alone. We need to keep the atmosphere clear
of all hindering spirits.

- **Do not** arrive late, unless entirely unavoidable. All the worshippers should start
  together and move forward together in unity,
  under the anointing of the Holy Spirit. The
  atmosphere of worship is disturbed by latecomers, especially in a small group. If a late
  arrival cannot be prevented, you should
  begin to worship in the car on the way, so as
  to be as much in the flow as possible upon
  entering the place of worship. Then just slip
  in and join with the other worshippers as
  seamlessly as possible.

- **Do not** depart from the flow of worship by
  movements "in the flesh"—such as walking
  over to check out the music, going in and
  out of doors, other than where unavoidable—
  as these movements are distracting to other
  worshippers and belong to the earthly realm,
  detracting from the heavenly realm that we
  are aspiring to. We do not want to dishonor
  the Holy Spirit by focusing on lesser things
  that can wait.

- **Do not** leave the leader(s) with the full
  responsibility of bringing heaven to earth,
  and pulling down the anointing, then judge
  them if you are not brought higher. Make
  every effort to enter in and be a participant

in drawing down the presence of the Lord.
He will be all the more blessed, and so, dear
worshipper, will you.

- **Do not** stand with hands in pockets while
  worshipping; this is not an attitude of wor-
  ship/praise! Hands should be free for raising
  and praising and offering and receiving.
  Hands in pockets is disrespectful of the
  most *high God*!

- **Do not** sit down, if this can be avoided.
  Sitting down usually involves a certain
  degree of disengagement from the worship
  and can alter the spiritual dynamic for all
  present, especially in a small group. If rest
  is absolutely needed, it is better to lie prone
  in His presence and allow yourself to be
  restored by the Holy Spirit.

- **Do not** pick up someone else's banners or
  shofar without their express permission, and
  do not be offended if they show reluctance
  to share their personal instruments of worship. This can be a sensitive issue. It is best if
  you have your own worship instruments.

- **Do not** leave banners lying on a chair or
  a pew or casually on the floor. Both com-
  munal and borrowed personal banners
  should be returned to the appointed place.
  Care should also be taken against crumpling
  and wrinkling, and against laying things on
  top of (especially) open banners, as soiling
  and wrinkles can be difficult or impossible

to remove. Even rolling up banners should
be done with care to avoid wrinkling, which
can be permanent.

Remember, the above "rules of thumb" are simply meant to heighten awareness of unconscious behavior that can hinder the anointing and thus compromise our corporate breakthrough worship. I invite you to consider these things, contemplate them, digest them, absorb them, appropriate those that speak to your circumstances; then forget them and enjoy the exhilaration and fruits of your breakthrough worship!

SCRIPTURAL POSTURES OF WORSHIP
(Authorized King James Version; emphases added)

And the man *bowed down his head, and worshipped* the LORD.

—GENESIS 24:26

And I *bowed down my head, and worshipped* the LORD...

—GENESIS 24:48

And it came to pass, that, when Abraham's servant heard their words, he *worshipped* the LORD, *bowing himself to the earth.*

—GENESIS 24:52

And the people believed: and when they heard that the LORD had visited the children of Israel, and that he had looked upon their affliction, then they *bowed their heads and worshipped.*

—EXODUS 4:31

That ye shall say, It is the sacrifice of the LORD's passover, who passed over the houses of the children of Israel in Egypt, when he smote the Egyptians, and delivered our houses. And the people *bowed the head and worshipped.*

—EXODUS 12:27

And all the people saw the cloudy pillar stand at the tabernacle door: and all the people *rose up and worshipped*, every man *in his tent door.*

—EXODUS 33:10

And Moses made haste, and *bowed his head toward the earth, and worshipped.*

—EXODUS 34:8

And he said, Nay; but as captain of the host of the LORD am I now come. And Joshua *fell on his face to the earth, and did worship…*

—JOSHUA 5:14

And when all the children of Israel saw how the fire came down, and the glory of the LORD upon the house, they *bowed themselves with their faces to the ground upon the pavement, and worshipped,* and praised the LORD, saying, For he is good; for his mercy endureth for ever.

—2 CHRONICLES 7:3

And Jehoshaphat *bowed his head with his face to the ground*: and all Judah and the inhabitants of Jerusalem *fell before the Lord, worshipping* the LORD.

—2 CHRONICLES 20:18

And when they had made an end of offering, *the king and all that were present with him bowed themselves, and worshipped.*

—2 CHRONICLES 29:29

And Ezra opened the book in the sight of all the people; (for he was above all the people;) and when he opened it, *all the people stood up:* And Ezra blessed the LORD, the great God. And all the people answered, Amen, Amen, with *lifting up their hands*: and *they bowed their heads, and worshipped* the LORD *with their faces to the ground.*

—NEHEMIAH 8:5–6

Then *stood up upon the stairs,* of the Levites [priests]…and *cried with a loud voice* unto the LORD their God. Then [other] Levites…said, *Stand up and bless* the LORD your God for ever and ever: and blessed be thy glorious name, which is exalted above all blessing and praise.

—NEHEMIAH 9:4–5

Then Job arose, and rent his mantle, and shaved his head, and *fell down upon the ground, and worshipped…*

—JOB 1:20

O come, let us *worship and bow down*: let us *kneel before the Lord* our maker.

—PSALM 95:6

Exalt ye the LORD our God, and *worship at his footstool*; for he is *holy.*

—PSALM 99:5

We will go into his tabernacles: we will *worship at his footstool.*

—PSALM 132:7

And when they [the wise men] were come into the house, they saw the young child with Mary his mother, and *fell down, and worshipped him…*

—MATTHEW 2:11

And [the devil] saith unto him [Jesus], All these things will I give thee, *if thou wilt fall down and worship me.* [The devil used the same model for worship to himself, indicating that this is the highest form of worship and therefore to be imitated.]

—MATTHEW 4:9

And as they went to tell his disciples, behold, Jesus met them, saying, All hail. And they came and *held him by the feet, and worshipped* him.

—MATTHEW 28:9

And they smote him on the head with a reed, and did spit upon him, and *bowing their knees worshipped him.* [Here a mocking gesture.]

—MARK 15:19

Behold, I will make them of the synagogue of Satan, which say they are Jews, and are not, but do lie; behold, I will make them to come and *worship before thy feet,* and to know that I have loved thee.

—REVELATION 3:9

The four and twenty elders *fall down before him* that sat on the throne, and worship him that liveth for ever and ever, *and cast their crowns before the throne,* saying, Thou art worthy, O Lord, to receive glory and honour and power: for thou hast created all things, and for thy pleasure they are and were created.

—REVELATION 4:10–11

And when he had taken the book, the four beasts and four and twenty elders *fell down before the Lamb,* having every one of them harps, and golden vials full of odours, which are the prayers of saints. And they sung a new song, saying, Thou art worthy…

—REVELATION 5:8–9

And the four beasts said, Amen. And the four and twenty *elders fell down and worshipped him* that liveth for ever and ever.

—REVELATION 5:14

And all the angels stood round about the throne, and about the elders and the four beasts, and *fell before the throne on their faces, and worshipped God,* Saying, Amen: Blessing, and glory, and wisdom, and thanksgiving, and honour, and power, and might, be unto our God for ever and ever.

—REVELATION 7:11–12

And the four and twenty elders, which sat before God on their seats, *fell upon their faces, and worshipped God,* Saying, We give thee thanks, O LORD God Almighty, which art, and wast, and art to come; because thou hast taken to thee thy great power, and hast reigned.

—REVELATION 11:16–17

And I John saw these things, and heard them. And when I had heard and seen, I *fell down to worship before the feet of the angel* which shewed me these things. Then saith he unto me, See thou *do it not:* for I am thy fellowservant, and of thy brethren the prophets, and of them which keep the sayings of this book: *worship God. [But the posture of worship was the same.]*

—REVELATION 22:8–9

ABOUT THE AUTHOR

DR. CYNTHIA DAY WALLACE is an international lawyer by profession, with a PhD from Cambridge University, specializing in international economic law. She has traveled and lectured globally in her specialized field and has lived in such capitals as Paris, Montreal, London, Vienna, Geneva, New York, and Washington DC. Her last professional position was a diplomatic post at the United Nations Economic Commission for Europe in Geneva, Switzerland. With over thirty legal publications, and national and international awards for both scholarly and creative writing, her international law books are on the syllabuses of leading universities around the world.

In Geneva Dr. Wallace was a co-founder, with two UN colleagues and associates, of an international church, where she then served as elder and intercessor, as well as on the music ministry and prayer ministry teams—at times leading worship, bringing a message from the pulpit, or speaking for a seminar. In 1997 she began monthly all-night prayer for Geneva, Israel, and the nations, which, by 2002, had evolved into weekly three- to five-hour prophetic intercessory worship nights that she named "Breakthrough Worship."

At the time of publication, Dr. Wallace is staying in

upstate New York, caring for her mother who is in her hundredth year. Her home otherwise remains a small Jura-mountain village outside and above Geneva where the "Breakthrough Worship" has been held over the last number of years in an historic 700-year-old church, once associated with the oldest *Chartreuse* (a type of monastery) in Switzerland.

With virtually every nation on the earth having a diplomatic presence in Geneva, the sense is that prayer over that city effectively reaches around the globe. It is Dr. Wallace's heart's desire to one day be able to claim the nations "for an inheritance."

BY THE SAME AUTHOR

**Don't Miss the Rapture: A Scriptural
Re-examination of the End-Time Scenario**
CREATION HOUSE, 2011, 336 PAGES.

**Foundations of the International Legal Rights
of the Jewish People and the State of Israel and the
Implications for the Proposed New Palestinian State**
CREATION HOUSE, 2012, 108 PAGES.

CONTACT THE AUTHOR

Website:
DrCDWallace.com

E-mail:
CDWALLACE@BLUEWIN.CH